'I believe this book to be the best on the market for sales training. Students find its practicality particularly useful. The information contained in this book is worth a fortune to any sales organisation because it allows the trainer to marry the enthusiasm of the rookie with the wisdom of the old hand.'
Jo Quilter, Director, QVQ Education Software

'By far the best book on selling I have ever read. I bought a copy for every member of my sales team. It is surely destined to be the definitive work on the subject.'
Guy Barber, Managing Director, TradersBazaar Promotions

'He understands his subject with a rare clarity and communicates it with a rare charm. This is surely the best book ever written on selling and I believe it will become a classic.'
Mike Richardson, Sales Manager, Top Line Parts

'Whatever your company sells, this book will help your sales team sell it better.'
David Cornish, Managing Director, Morgan Stewart Recruitment

'The tips, tricks and techniques described in this book amount to uncommon wisdom. It is without doubt the Rolls Royce of sales books.'
Chris Dadd, Senior Manager, Win Telecommunications Services

'There must be a huge market for a book that can turn average consultants into sales stars and this is just such a book. It is also entertaining, informative and human. The charm is there from beginning to end.'
Wayne Preece, Services Sales Executive, Microsoft (UK)

'This book is a guide, a perfect guide, to how to win in selling. It covers everything you will ever need to know to sell ethically and successfully and it is wonderfully comprehensive.'
Ronnie McCrorie, Head of Sales, Syntel Europe

'Common sense is an uncommon thing. This book has it, and it knows how to apply it to increase sales.'
Chris Piff, Contracts Manager, DÄB Lighting

'The information in this book does not date, translates to all countries and is useful to all salespeople. It covers everything you could wish to know about selling.'
Andrew Foxcroft, Managing Director, Trusted Business Intelligence

KT-559-913

The Secrets
of Selling

The Secrets
of Selling

How to win in any sales situation

Geoff King

FT Prentice Hall
FINANCIAL TIMES

An imprint of **Pearson Education**

Harlow, England • London • New York • Boston • San Francisco • Toronto
Sydney • Tokyo • Singapore • Hong Kong • Seoul • Taipei • New Delhi
Cape Town • Madrid • Mexico City • Amsterdam • Munich • Paris • Milan

PEARSON EDUCATION LIMITED

Edinburgh Gate
Harlow CM20 2JE
Tel: +44 (0)1279 623623
Fax: +44 (0)1279 431059
Website: www.pearsoned.co.uk

First published in Great Britain in 2007

ISBN: 978-0-273-71300-5

British Library Cataloguing-in-Publication Data
A catalogue record for this book is available from the British Library

Library of Congress Cataloging-in-Publication Data
A catalog record for this book is available from the Library of Congress

10 9 8 7 6 5 4 3
11 10 09 08

Typeset in 9.5/13pt in Din Regular by 30
Printed and bound in Great Britain by Ashford Colour Press, Gosport

The publisher's policy is to use paper manufactured from sustainable forests.

This book is dedicated to my wife Laura.
When I first met you I fell in love,
and you smiled because you knew.

Contents

Acknowledgements

We are grateful to the following for permission to reproduce copyright material:

Figure 1 in chapter 1 from Baron, Robert A. and Byrne, Don R., *Social Psychology: Understanding Human Interaction*, 1st edn. Published by Allyn and Bacon, Boston, MA. Copyright © 1994 by Pearson Education. Reprinted by permission of the publisher.

Microsoft product screen shot on p.167 reprinted with permission from Microsoft Corporation.

In some instances we have been unable to trace the owners of copyright material, and we would appreciate any information that would enable us to do so.

Introduction
So what is this book about and how will it help you?

'Every man who got where he is, has had to begin where he was.'

Robert Louis Stevenson (1850–94), novelist

The rules of selling rarely change. In most areas of business, fashions and buzzwords come and go, but in selling there is a gold standard that changes little over time. This book describes that gold standard for you. Once learnt, it will stay with you for life.

This book gives you advice for selling in any situation. Advice that is useful and practical but not commonly applied. It contains no management jargon, so you will not find a single reference to paradigm shifts, strategic refocusing, framework leveraging or any other such business speak. It just has the skills you need to sell well. The tips, tricks and techniques to win in any sales situation.

Selling is probably the hardest part of your career but also the part which, when done as it should be done, will most benefit that career. If you had to gain all that experience yourself it would take, at best, several years in optimum circumstances and it would cost a lot to do. Not least in lost sales. This book condenses all that knowledge, allowing you to reach that gold standard sooner.

It is also useful for those who do not sell products and services directly. This is because almost everyone sells in some sense and at some time.

There is a lot in here that will show you how to be more persuasive to other people. This book will also reveal to you what salespeople are doing when they sell to you.

The examples cover a whole range of products and services, so what your company sells may well be mentioned. But even if what you sell is not here, the way to sell it certainly will be. Because while the things that people sell vary greatly over time, the way to sell them changes little.

The Secrets of Selling is divided into three parts. The first deals with sales meetings and sales proposals, which is the area where most people first get involved in selling. The second shows you the most effective methods for winning new work – not just from existing clients, but from new ones too. The third part gives advice for all the special situations you may encounter so that you are prepared for them when they happen.

You probably have a lot of things to do today, but why not put them aside for one moment and turn the page over instead. Because there are things in this book that are very valuable to you ...

PART 1

'The meeting of preparation with opportunity
generates the offspring that we call luck.'

Anthony Robbins (b. 1960), motivational speaker

SALES MEETINGS AND SALES PROPOSALS

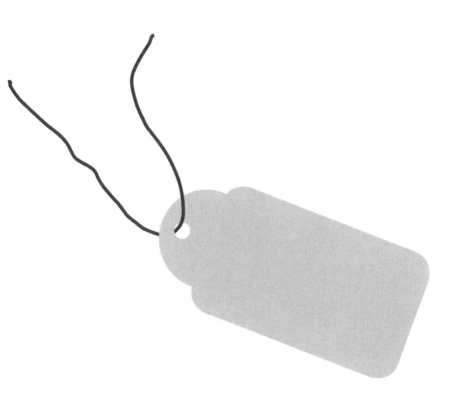

Chapter **1**

What to say in sales meetings

- Preparing for sales meetings
- The structure of a typical sales meeting
- Dealing with objections
- Closing

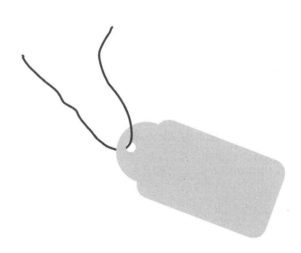

'Give every man your ear, but few your voice.'
Shakespeare (1564–1616), poet and playwright

Preparing for sales meetings

1 TIP ONE: Plan what your prospect can give you

Most salespeople, when planning a meeting, make the mistake of planning the agenda. In other words they plan what *will be discussed* during the meeting. A better approach is to plan what you would like your prospect *to give you* during the meeting.

So what could the prospect give you? There are rarely more than six things a prospect can give you. They are:

> The contract itself, or a pilot for it.

> The knowledge that you should walk away, knowing you cannot win the sale.

> A timeline on which to base the sale.

> A schedule of dates at which you both meet to review progress on work .

> A who's-who chart of the organisation.

> Other help to explore the account (sometimes known as a 'hunting licence').

You need to ask yourself which of these you should look to win.

2 TIP TWO: Find out about the prospect's company

There is no need to trawl through pages of company accounts to do this. What you want are the main themes and issues in the company. In medium to large companies most, or all, of the main issues will be in the public domain. Indeed the larger the company is, the easier it is to establish what these issues must be. An efficient way to do this is to contact the *Financial Times* annual results service and ask for a copy of that company's annual report to be posted to you. The directors' summary at the beginning of the annual report will outline the issues you need to know. This service is free and can be contacted on ++44 20 8391 6000 or www.ft.annualreports.com

3 TIP THREE: Anticipate what will be discussed in the meeting

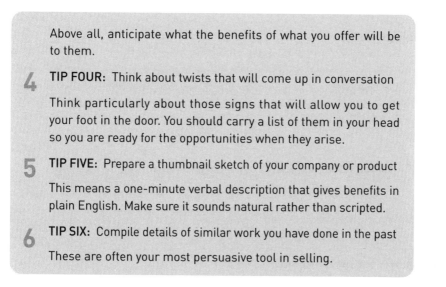

Above all, anticipate what the benefits of what you offer will be to them.

4 **TIP FOUR:** Think about twists that will come up in conversation

Think particularly about those signs that will allow you to get your foot in the door. You should carry a list of them in your head so you are ready for the opportunities when they arise.

5 **TIP FIVE:** Prepare a thumbnail sketch of your company or product

This means a one-minute verbal description that gives benefits in plain English. Make sure it sounds natural rather than scripted.

6 **TIP SIX:** Compile details of similar work you have done in the past

These are often your most persuasive tool in selling.

First impressions – the three twelves

You already know how important first impressions are, but do you know how to maximise your chances of making a good first impression? Well, there is a salesperson's adage that sums it up neatly. The adage is called the 'three twelves' and it refers to:

1 the first 12 words you say
2 the first 12 footsteps you take
3 the top 12 inches of your appearance (i.e. from your shoulders up).

The first part of the adage – the first 12 words you say – means you must ensure that the first words you say are about the prospect, not about yourself. People are quick to judge.

The second part – about footsteps – refers to the dangers of crowding someone in. It means you need to give them space as you walk into their room.

The part about the top 12 inches (30 cm) refers to the way people judge smartness because there is a trick to appearing smart. The trick is to focus on the top 12 inches of your appearance because that is where the other person will focus. By comparison, they will hardly notice the rest of you. (Although shoes can be an exception to this rule.)

Smartness is an important attribute in selling because people subconsciously associate a smartly dressed salesperson with a higher quality product or service. Think of a situation where the exact same item of clothing is sold both in an upmarket Paris shop and in a backstreet market. Most people will perceive the one in the upmarket shop to be of higher quality.

But what if your prospects all wear casual clothes in their office? A good rule of thumb is that a salesperson should always dress 'one level above' the prospect in terms of smartness. This rule applies whether your work takes you to the air-conditioned elegance of Sydney's Pitt Street or the baking heat of the outback. Always dress 'one level above'.

Arriving late

If you think you might be one or two minutes late for a meeting it is tempting to believe there is no need to call ahead and tell the prospect you are running late. Such thoughts are comforting at the time, but they just store up problems for later. It is always best to phone ahead if you are going to be late, and few people will mind that lateness so long as they are told in advance. However, when people are kept waiting and you have not phoned ahead, they tend to spend the time they are kept waiting dwelling on your faults.

So let us assume you have got to the meeting on time and you made a good first impression. What should you do now?

The structure of a typical sales meeting

In a sales meeting you cannot force someone to agree with you. Rather you should let them get *your* own way. To do that, you first need to understand how a good sales meeting is structured. The best meetings follow this structure:

> **The introduction:** The prospect gains a rapport with you, and a belief that you may be able to help.

> **The consultation/questioning:** The largest part of most sales.

> **The check questions:** There to ensure you have not missed anything.

> **The selling:** When you match the features of what you offer to the buyer's needs and create a meeting of minds.

> **Asking for the business:** Often called closing.

Now we will look at each of these sections in detail.

The introduction

There are three things you need to achieve in an introduction:

> You need to get yourself accepted on a personal level. The reason for this is that people much prefer to buy from people they like. This aspect of human character is examined in more detail in Chapter 3 (on using emotion in selling).

> You need to get the prospect to believe you can help them. Before you contacted them they may well have concluded that their issue was unsolvable. You need to provide them with a realistic hope.

> You need to induce a mindset in which the prospect feels they can open up to you.

A thumbnail sketch of your company

So how do you get them to open up? Often, a good start is to open up yourself first (but without dominating the conversation). The point of this is not so much to tell the other party about your company. Rather, by opening up a little about your company you can get them to open up about themselves. Therefore you need to prepare a short description of your company – a thumbnail sketch.

Test your sketch beforehand It is important that you sound smooth and natural when delivering your sketch, so you will need to practise it. You will know you have it sorted when you are able to give clear, succinct and natural sounding answers to the following questions:

> What does your company do?

> What are the benefits of what you offer?

These questions are deceptively simple. Providing top-flight answers to them takes thought and preparation.

The consultation/questioning

The aim of this phase of the sale is to achieve a situation in which the conversation between the two parties is completely open and fluid. Psychologists call this state 'flow'. Professor Mihaly Csikszentmihalyi of Claremont Graduate University, California is widely regarded as the world's leading psychologist on this subject. Having studied it for many years, he described flow as

> *Being completely involved in an activity for its own sake. The ego falls away. Time flies. Every action, movement, and thought follows inevitably from the previous one, like playing jazz. Your whole being is involved, and you're using your skills to the utmost.*

This state is something you often see in people who are leaders in their field – world-class athletes or musicians for example. Their best performances often seem to have an effortless and flowing quality that sets them apart from their peers. If you can get your prospect into such a state, one in which they talk openly and freely about their situation, then opportunities are certain to arise. That is why the best salespeople seem more consultant than salesperson. But how can you achieve flow in the bustle of a typical meeting? Well, it is a lot to do with listening ...

So how do you listen well?

We saw earlier that a key to selling is not to sell to a prospect but to make them want to buy. Think about it. You know when you are being 'sold to' and the chances are you resent the pressure that goes with it. However, buying is a genuine pleasure – particularly when the person selling to you is taking a genuine interest in your situation. A lot of the difference between these two experiences is down to listening.

Few people are naturally good at listening, but it is a skill that can easily be improved. It really boils down to the following:

> ➤ You should remember that you have two ears and one mouth and you should use them in that ratio. Very few salespeople achieve this and that means the prospect feels they are being *talked at* rather than *listened to*. Listening is what makes the difference between selling and telling.

> ➤ Don't think about your troubles during the conversation, think about theirs.

> ➤ Let them tell their story first and let them tell everything. Listen to the emotion in their story and don't interrupt them. Think about your visits to your doctor. Wouldn't you find it bizarre if the doctor did not ask you about your symptoms but, as soon as you stepped into the room, talked to you about the wonderful features of a new pill and suggested you take that pill? (Put like that it sounds bizarre, but it is what a lot of salespeople do.)

> ➤ Do not use the time in which your prospect is talking to prepare what you are going to say next. Instead, use that time to listen. This

is another of the differences between talking *with* someone and talking *at* them.

> Don't judge them. Just accept what they say.

> Concentrate on the conversation. Avoid thinking about other things.

> Do not think about the money you will earn from the sale while you are in the prospect's company. The prospect will pick up on your thoughts. You will have time to count the money later.

> Watch that their body language matches what they are saying. If it does not, you have found something that needs probing.

> The two best questions you have at your disposal are 'What do you mean exactly?' and 'How do you feel about that?' 'What do you mean exactly' is an excellent way to probe a subject more deeply. You will feel awkward when you first use it but it will soon come naturally. 'How do you feel about that?' is explored in more detail in the next chapter.

> The word 'situation' is a great word to use when questioning. It allows the prospect to explain how they got to where they are without ascribing blame. It avoids the word 'problem', which has negative connotations.

> Where possible, you should ask questions that lead towards your strengths and the competitor's weaknesses.

> You need to discover the prospect's true buying motives and that means approaching the meeting with a general or horizontal knowledge of the subject rather than a specific or vertical knowledge. The following analogy helps explain this. Imagine a shop assistant works in a sports shop and a middle-aged man comes in. The man announces that he is taking up golf and wants to buy some golf equipment. It would help the sale greatly if the assistant knew his true buying motives – his real reasons for taking up golf. The chances are those motives are to do with a desire for a hobby, for exercise or for meeting new people. Horizontal knowledge will lead you to ask questions that expose those buying motives. Questions such as 'How often do you expect to be playing?' 'Will you be playing competitively?' 'Is the brand name of the club important to you?' and so on. The danger with too much vertical knowledge in one specialist area is that the assistant plunges straight in with something like a technical analysis of the finer points of golf club design. A sure way to kill the sale.

> Use open questions to open the prospect up, and closed questions to close them down. (Open questions start with one of the six

pronouns: who, what, when, where, why and how. Closed questions start with verbs.)

> Remember you can be quite pushy while maintaining a consultative approach. The trick is to be politely pushy. Nothing masks pushiness better than being polite. It is noticeable that many top salespeople mask a go-getting nature behind an easy and courteous manner.

Let them stew a little in their problems By now the prospect should be describing their situation in a free and open way. As they do so, you should hold back from suggesting solutions. What is needed at this point is for the prospect to sit there, outlining their problems to you.

The chances are the prospect knew about these problems before they met you. However, they did not reach a solution the last time they thought about them so the problems were compartmentalised and became latent problems. As they describe the problems to you again the old issues will resurface and they will feel the pain of those problems again.

Build a relationship while you are listening This is the part of the sale in which you have the greatest opportunity to build a relationship with the prospect. If you adopt a consultative approach you will make the whole process a more pleasant experience for them. This is the approach of a good doctor, or a good TV interviewer, and it is exactly the manner you should adopt.

Get it in writing

You should also make copious notes during the listening phase of the sale because you may have to submit a written proposal in the future. If you do, the quality of your proposal will be closely tied to the quality of the notes you took in the meeting. You should make those notes with a smart pen rather than a cheap ballpoint. The reason for this is the same as the reason for dressing smartly – people subconsciously associate a smart salesperson with a higher quality offering. Also, make sure you always use a pad to write your notes on. It avoids marking the prospect's furniture.

As you approach the end of the listening stage you should have a clear understanding of the prospect's situation and their buying motives. On top of that, the prospect will be feeling the full pain of their problem.

We are nearly at the point where they are most receptive to possible solutions. But it is not, quite yet, time for us to offer those solutions.

The check questions

It is often the case in life that you need to finish one stage of something completely before you can move on to the next stage, and it is the same with selling. Before moving on from the consultation stage you need to check that you have a sound understanding of the prospect's situation. If you are ever tempted to leave the check questions out, just remember that the prospect will find it disconcerting if they are not asked. For them, it would be rather like seeing that doctor again who this time asked about the symptoms but did not check they had covered everything before prescribing the cure.

Check questions need not be elaborate. Something like 'Are you absolutely sure we have covered everything?' Or 'Is there anything we could have missed?' Once you are satisfied with the answers to your check questions you are ready to go on to the next stage.

Check questions only take a moment and in the time it takes to ask them the prospect will not lose any of their desire to buy. Rather, it is more usual for their desire to increase at this point.

The selling

It is at this stage, and only this stage, that you actually start selling. So what is the best way to go about that? Well, the core of it is to match your company's strengths to your prospect's buying motives. This is where you match things up and tie things together. Here is how you do that effectively.

Don't sell the feature, sell the benefit

Features and benefits are simple concepts, but often overlooked. Here are two examples that highlight the difference between them.

Imagine that a customer walks into a hardware shop and asks for a drill. The point here is that the customer does not really want a drill. What he really wants is a hole. The drill is the feature, the hole is the benefit. Now imagine a person walking into a bank to ask about a mortgage. The feature she is asking for is to chain herself to debt for 25 years. The benefit is that she can buy a home.

Features on their own do little to sell. But benefits can be very persuasive.

Features to sell products Salespeople usually do better at explaining the benefits of a product's features than at explaining those of a service. For example, they might explain how ABS brakes are put on a car to benefit the driver's safety. The only time that features of products are difficult to sell is when new technology is concerned. For example, texting is very popular now but its benefits must have been difficult to sell when it was first introduced. (The answer would have been to tell customers they are able to receive texts on their phone.)

Features to sell services Some features and benefits come up very frequently when selling services so you should be fully conversant with them. Here are the most common ones:

Feature: Your firm has strong project management disciplines.
Benefit: These disciplines give greater clarity and certainty to the client than would otherwise be the case.

Feature: Your firm has strong experience of the prospect's industry sector.
Benefit: Technical prowess is most valuable when tied to business application and that is exactly what your company is offering here.

Feature: Your firm is a specialist in the technical field in question.
Benefit: Specialists are more likely to deliver a good job than generalists.

Simple, isn't it? So why is such a simple practice so frequently overlooked?

Well, the answer lies in a common and very human weakness: making false assumptions about other people. What happens in a typical sale is that the salesperson describes a feature of what they offer and *assumes* the prospect will understand from that description what the benefit is. Put another way, the salesperson believes that, simply by mentioning the feature, the prospect will straight away see the associated benefit. However, a lot of prospects just do not make that connection. One reason they do not is that they just are not that interested in the features. They are interested in the benefits. People tend to listen more attentively to what they are interested in.

So how do you ensure you always mention benefit statements when you should? A failsafe way is to do this is that whenever you describe a feature of what you offer you should say to yourself 'which means that'. The next words you say will describe the benefit.

Now we need to return to other advice for this stage of the sale. The stage at which a meeting of minds takes place.

Appeal to their self-interest, but not too overtly

You are usually on safe ground by appealing to another person's self inter- est. Indeed it is usually the best approach. There are, however, two potential problems to be aware of. The first is that by appealing to base motives you can cause yourself to appear base. (Remember, people prefer to buy from someone they like.) The second is that an appeal to higher motives can, on occasion, be very potent. For example, people will some- times choose one company over another because of green credentials.

A good example of appealing to higher motives was provided by the British politician Sir Winston Churchill with his phrase 'I have nothing to offer but blood, sweat, toil and tears'. Politicians are not usually that honest. And they are not usually that persuasive either. The persuasion came from an appeal to a higher motive.

What a difference a word makes Human beings are sensitive and politi- cal creatures and therefore too many ill-chosen words can break a sale. The effect is similar to untuning a number of notes on a piano and thereby creating discord throughout a whole song. No one expects all your words to be perfect. It is just that you should not use too many discordant ones.

It is during the meeting-of-minds stage of a sale that your prospect is most sensitive to the words you use. Therefore you should use words that ease the client towards saying 'yes'. We have already seen this effect with 'situation' and 'problem'. Here are some other common examples:

> Do not say 'cost', say 'amount'.

> Do not say 'contract', say 'agreement'.

> Do not say 'pitch', say 'presentation'.

> Do not say 'buy', say 'authorise'.

> Do not say 'cheap', say 'value for money'.

> Do not say 'change', say 'improve'.

A particular word to avoid is 'solution' because it is one of the most unin- formative and overused words in business. It can also imply that the person using it has a shallow understanding of the subject being dis- cussed.

Be succinct People listen to what we say a lot less than we think they do. Your best defence against this is to be succinct in what you say. Two leading researchers in this field are Robert Baron and Don Byrne. They looked at a broad spectrum of human communications and concluded that listening just isn't something that comes easily for most of us. They devised the following diagram:

FIGURE 1

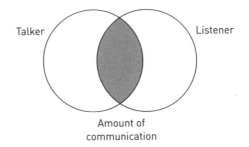

People listen less than you think

Talker   Listener

Amount of
communication

From Baron, Robert A. and Byrne, Don R., *Social Psychology: Understanding Human Interaction*, 1st edn. Published by Allyn and Bacon, Boston, MA. Copyright © 1994 by Pearson Education. Reprinted by permission of the publisher.

Use their name (sparingly) People listen more closely if you put their name into the conversation from time to time. Just avoid overdoing it.

Dealing with objections (and false objections)

A sale cannot happen until an objection has been overcome. Quite simply there is something in human nature that means an objection *must* be overcome before a sale can be made. A person who says 'yes' throughout the conversation but never raises an objection will end up not buying.

In selling it does not matter whether the objection is real or imagined. It is just that human nature requires there to be an objection and requires that objection to be overcome.

The best way to coax out objections is to adopt an open and consultative manner that welcomes them. You will find you need to clear one level of objections fully before you can tackle the next level.

False objections People often raise objections that you know are false. They are not doing this for any offbeat reason; rather, it is another common trait of human nature. (The most common false objection is for a prospect to say they need to run a decision past someone else when in fact they are the decision maker.)

The most common causes of false objections are that the prospect wants time to think or time to catch up with the conversation. When a prospect raises a real objection you have to overcome it. When they raise a false objection you can politely ignore it and move on. Of course that begs the question of how you will know whether an objection is real or false? Well, you will probably know when you hear the objection, but if in doubt the following test will help you. False objections are only raised once. Real objections come up persistently until they are fully dealt with. False objections occur more frequently at the beginning of a sale. The objections made towards the end are nearly always real.

So what are the real objections you may face?

Assuming the prospect has a desire for what you offer, the objections will probably come down to one or more of the following five:

> Your company does not have the best set of skills or products.
> The prospect knows of other companies better placed to do the work.
> The prospect has a personal dislike of you or your company.
> The prospect turns out not to be the real decision maker.
> The prospect thinks it costs too much.

Obviously it makes sense to prepare your answers to these objections. Here are some standard answers to each one.

Your company does not have the best set of skills or products The only defence to this objection is to see it coming and make arrangements such that you do have the right skills and products in place. For example, you might need to partner with a third-party firm in order to win a particular contract.

The prospect knows of other companies better placed to do the work There is little you can do to counter this objection. When it appears you should probably cut your losses and move to the next prospect.

The prospect has a personal dislike of you or your company This objection cannot be cured, only prevented. You need to head it off before it happens by ensuring that they like you from the beginning.

The prospect turns out not to be the real decision maker This is really about you getting access to power and that is an area best covered in the questioning stage of the sale. Of course there will be times when the prospect is a key influencer of the decision but does not have the ultimate sign-off. What to do in these situations is examined in Chapter 17 – (tips on managing large accounts).

The prospect thinks it costs too much When price is an objection you should not tackle it in earnest until all the other objections have been sorted. You need to reach the point at which price is the only thing stopping the prospect from buying. Once you reach that point the conversation will become a straightforward negotiation on price and that is a negotiation you should be able to win.

However, that does not mean you should leave the price as some great climax to your presentation. Rather, you should avoid deep discussion of it until the prospect has a reasonable understanding of what your company provides. The reason is that when price is first mentioned prospects will, on average, think the price should be 40–50 per cent of what you say. This is a situation that needs to be managed and that means introducing the price gently as you progress through the sale.

Be proud of your price. Some consultants have an issue with the 'selling' of their daily rate and that often shows through to the prospect. The solution is to remember the following key truth: when selling your own time it is not the price of your time that matters, it is the value it gives to the client. If you are giving more value to the client than you are taking in fees then your price is unlikely to be a problem.

Once you have asked all the check questions and cleared all the objections the sale is yours for the asking. But how should you ask for it?

Asking for the business

This really comes down to three things. When to ask, what to say and how to say it.

When to ask

In most sales you will feel the conversation move to a point where a close is the natural next step. However, there will be times when you want to look for tangible signals to support that intuition. Those signals will be either verbal or visual:

> **Verbal buying signals:** A verbal buying signal is something said by the prospect that shows they are interested in what you offer. For example, questions like 'When could you start?' or 'How much would it cost?' Often the prospect will miss the implication of their question. Make sure you don't.

> **Visual buying signals:** There is one classic visual sign that means it is time to ask for the business. When a prospect straightens their fingers and lets the fingertips touch (often called steepling) they are giving you a very clear signal, because people subconsciously adopt this posture when they are on the cusp of a decision. Next time you find yourself steepling your fingers, why not pause to check your thoughts at that moment. The chances are you will be on just such a cusp.

FIGURE 2

Steepled fingers

One final point about the timing of a close. There will still be a few occasions when you just do not know if it is time to ask for the business. At such times, and if you think you have half a chance of winning, you should just steel yourself and ask for the business. As Wayne Gretzky, a top Canadian ice hockey player puts it 'You miss 100 per cent of the shots you never take'.

So much for when to close. Next we need to look at what to say.

What to say

There are a number of things you can say to close a sale, and you may have used many of them in the past without fully realising what you said. The common factor to all of them is that they ask for the business with finesse rather than bluntness. The main closes are:

Closing on a minor issue This is a particularly useful close for professional service sales. It may be that you expect the total billing for a project to top £5 million, but the project is effectively closed by an agreement that a senior consultant will do a few weeks work on the first parts of it. All you need to do is suggest a time when that senior consultant can do those few weeks.

In the mid-1970s the psychologists Robert Cialdini and David Scroeder, based at the University of Arizona, tested the effectiveness of this close and found it to be approximately 1.75 times more effective than a straightforward request for the work. The reason it works is that it effectively sidesteps the problem of inertia. The larger the deal the more inertia there is and the more people hesitate before committing. Psychologically, it is much easier to commit to a small deal. You only need a small deal to get the project underway.

The alternative close This is usually a suggestion along the lines of 'I could arrange the start date/delivery for either the 18th or 25th of this month. Which would be better for you?' You are asking them to choose between alternatives. Either choice closes the sale.

The assumptive close This close deliberately assumes the prospect wants what you are offering. It is typically phrased along the lines of 'It looks like everything is agreed. I will get our team together and they can start promptly.' Obviously this close requires a note of confidence to your voice and confidence is a great persuader. You just have to be careful not to over do it. Confidence sells but arrogance repels.

The checking availability close This close starts with you saying something like 'Let me just check whether that particular consultant is available'. You then, of course, make the check, confirm the availability and thereby close the sale.

The conditional close This is where you bring the decision down to one final condition. 'If I could arrange that for you would you be happy for us to do the work?' Or, 'If I could do it for that price would you be happy to go ahead?' Of course this close only works when you know that just one obstacle remains.

The invitational close This is usually something like 'Why don't we try this for a month with no strings attached? If you feel after that that you would like to work with us, we can look at a more formal agreement.'

But what if none of the above works? Then there are two options left open to you.

The Ben Franklin close This decision-making method is named after the American statesman and inventor who is believed to have devised it. Whether he actually did or not, he certainly popularised it. His method consisted of drawing a line down the middle of a piece of paper. On one side he wrote the reasons in favour of a particular action. On the other side, the reasons against.

This method is a close in its own right. You simply explain it to your prospect and volunteer to fill in one of the columns – the one that lists the reasons why they should buy. Then ask them to fill in the other column. Your list will usually be more persuasive.

The final offer close Your chances of selling are highest if you can get the prospect to agree to the deal while you are with them. However, the spectrum of human character has many colours and you will have some prospects who simply refuse to be closed on the spot. They can take up a lot of your time.

In these circumstances the best move is to leave them a copy of the agreement signed by you, with a clearly marked space for them to sign, and then leave a reply paid envelope. Depending on your industry sector, about 20 per cent of these agreements will be signed and posted back to you. But only use this method if you really have to. It is a last resort.

How to say it

There are many books that portray closing as some mysterious skill that is half art and half hypnotic magic. Other books portray it as a matter of persistence. In this second school of thought the sale is a boxing match in which you are sure to win if you just keep hitting the other person's fist with your head.

Done properly, closing has little resemblance to either scenario. There are just two rules about *how* to close:

1 **RULE ONE:** Ask for the work

You must actually ask for the work. People expect it of you and they will feel uncomfortable if you do not ask, or dance around the question.

2 **RULE TWO:** Keep quiet

Once you have asked for the business you must *shut up*!

It is a simple technique but silence from you at this point will exert a remarkable psychological pressure on the prospect. Curiously, whoever speaks first after the request for business has been made will nearly always 'lose'. So long as you keep your nerve, the chances are strongly in favour of you winning. It really is that simple.

Perhaps you feel cynical that such a simple technique could be so powerful? Why not test it for yourself the next time you feel you have made a good pitch? When you first try this, time will seem to hang in the air and the silence will be oppressive. It will make you feel uncomfortable but you *must* resist the temptation to break the silence. Keep quiet and you will probably win.

Two tips for selling to groups

You could be forgiven for thinking that the psychology of selling to a group or committee is so hopelessly complex that there is no point in studying it. Actually, it is surprisingly simple. The way to decipher the thought processes of a group is to watch the body language. There are two things to look for.

1 **TIP ONE:** Focus on the senior person

Before you start the sale you will usually know which person is the senior figure in the group. This is because people generally give their job titles when they are making introductions. The trick when selling to groups is to focus your efforts on the senior person in the group. The other people in the group will almost always follow their lead. If you win over the senior person, you will win the others over too.

There may of course be times when you present while knowing little about your audience. When this happens you can usually spot the senior figure by looking for the person from whom everyone takes their lead.

2 **TIP TWO:** Focus on the waverers

This method is just as simple. Any group of people, whatever activity they are engaged in, will naturally divide into three groups: a progressive group, a conservative group and a wavering group. The waverers hold the power here, and the trick to winning is to focus on the waverers. Indeed, if you look at most western countries you will see that elections are nearly always won by the party that most closely appeals to the positive aspirations of the floating voters. Exactly the same holds true in business.

That nearly concludes what you need to know for sales meetings. There is just one more point to add ...

Use the meeting to get another meeting

Once your meeting has come to an end it is worth asking the prospect if they know of anyone else in the company you should be talking to. The point is this. Once you have met one person in a company it is a lot easier to meet the second. Success builds success and you should capitalise on it.

Most people will be happy to give you the name of another contact within the company and your question will come at a time when they have a clear idea of what your company does. Doing this saves you a lot of prospecting time.

Of course, you will do a lot better in meetings if you can quickly gauge the character of your prospect, and that is what the next chapter is about ...

Chapter **2**

How to assess the character of your prospect quickly and accurately

- How to make these judgements
- The most common reasons why people misjudge the characters of others

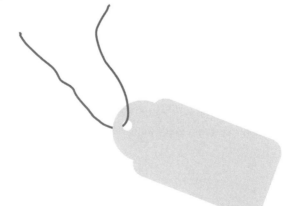

'You must look into people, as well as at them.'
Lord Chesterfield (1694–1773), correspondent

It is natural to assume that other people see things the way we do. However, if you present a group of people with a straightforward piece of information they usually have very different reactions to that information. (Think how journalists, presented with the same information, report it so differently.) Imagine the sales advantage you would have if you knew in advance how each individual prospect would react to a given piece of information.

It is very easy to gain that advantage. Here's how.

The need to judge others quickly and correctly

There are many methods by which you can understand a person's character. Most of them work by checking for particular traits in that person's character, because when such a trait is identified it is usually possible to predict how that will react in specific situations. The chief failing of these methods is that psychologists have now identified nearly 5,000 personality traits. One human simply cannot do that many checks in the first few minutes of meeting another human. There is just too much information to process in too short a time; too many colours in the spectrum.

What you need is a quick, easy-to-use method that gives you a reliable and accurate diagnosis of a person's character when you first meet them. Fortunately, there is such a method. It works by concentrating your analysis on just two of those 5,000-plus influences that affect human character. The method is simple to use and delivers accurate results. The reason it works is that it focuses on just the two strongest traits of human character. The two that most affect human character.

Specifically, the method involves you judging where a person's character sits on two scales. Once you have judged the correct position on each scale, you will understand approximately 80 per cent of their character. That is all you need do. Here are those two scales:

> The first scale determines the degree to which someone is introverted or extroverted. Psychologists see this as the single most significant measure of human character. You have to judge where on this scale a person sits.

FIGURE 1

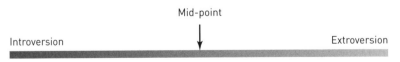

The second scale determines the degree to which someone is task-oriented or people-oriented. Psychologists see this as the second most significant measure of human behaviour. (Task-oriented people tend to be logical, objective and analytical. The people-oriented tend to be more emotional, subjective and personal.) Again, you judge where on this scale the person sits.

FIGURE 2

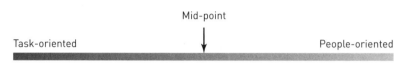

Mid-point

Task-oriented   People-oriented

By combining the two results you can then place the person on the following chart.

The building blocks of modern psychology: the four main ways people behave

FIGURE 3

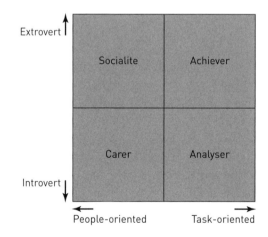

This method of defining character was first developed by Hippocrates (460 BC – 377 BC) He was the first to notice that people nearly always behave in one of four ways. Despite its age, no better method for quickly defining character has yet been invented. Indeed, this part of his work is still the building block for most modern psychology.

The reason this test works so well is that it allows you to put the detail to one side and concentrate on the big picture. You only need to be with a person for a few moments to make a sound judgement as to where they are on these two scales, but once you know that, you can predict their behaviour very accurately.

Here is a summary of these four personality types – each of the four squares – and how they typically behave.

Type 1, Achiever: Extrovert and task-oriented

FIGURE 4

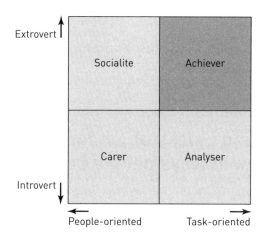

Psychologists call these people choleric, or Type A personalities. They tend to be competitive and achieving, strong-willed, assertive and purposeful. Henry Ford, the founder of the car-making firm, is a classic example of this temperament. So are many leaders in business and military affairs. These people are in many ways natural leaders.

So what makes them want to buy? A key driver for these people is that they want to get things done, they want them done now, and they want them done well. If you focus on that desire when communicating with them, they will find you a compelling salesperson.

Type 2, Analyser: Introvert and task-oriented

FIGURE 5

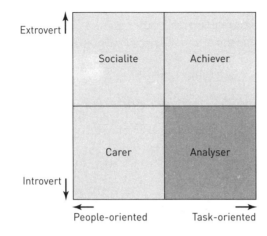

Termed 'phlegmatic' in psychology, these are cool and detached types who are more observers of the world than participants in it. Caution and self-discipline are key traits for them and they have a tendency to be formal and precise. Typical careers for such people would be as accountants or forensic investigators. A classic example of this character is Sherlock Holmes.

So what makes them want to buy? Arguments that are heavily influenced by logic and factual data.

Type 3, Socialite: Extrovert and people-oriented

FIGURE 6

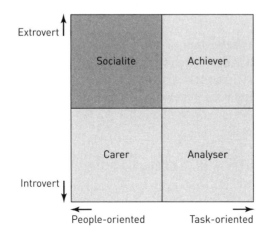

Also termed 'sanguine', typically these people are sociable, optimistic and enthusiastic. They like to be liked and are poor at objective judgement. They are expressive, persuasive and cheerful. Many famous singers and actors have personalities of this type (think of Eddie Murphy, the American comedian). In business they feature prominently in sales, marketing and promotions.

So what makes them want to buy? These people are best persuaded by arguments that focus on social acceptance because getting approval from other people is always an important consideration in their decision-making. They look to bring along everyone with the decision. These people find enthusiasm very persuasive and that is the hook you should use when selling to them.

Type 4, Carer: Introvert and people-oriented

FIGURE 7

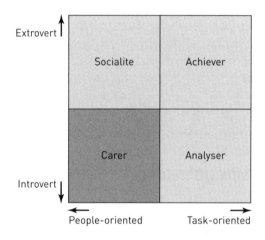

Psychologists call this group 'melancholic'. They tend to be caring and loyal but lacking in drive. Typically, they are patient and steady characters who prefer close relationships with a small number of people to loose relationships with many. There are few well-known examples of this type because they tend to shun the limelight. In day-to-day life you often meet them in technical or caring roles.

So what makes them want to buy? Melancholic people are particularly adverse to two things: change and risk. They want lasting solutions that will defend them from these two 'dangers'. To sell well to them, you need to slant your arguments accordingly.

Most people find this method useful for approximately 80 per cent of the people they meet in business situations. Of course, all methods have their flaws. The main flaw with this one is that it is of limited use when you meet a person whose character lies at the centre of both axes.

At this point in the book you should pause for a moment and think about where your character fits on this chart. As the ancient Greeks put it: first know thyself. Once you have done that, think about some of the people you know. Then try placing them on the chart. These processes will help cement the concept in your mind.

Once you are practised with this system you will notice that you find it much easier to relate to people in the same quadrant as yourself. You will also relate, although to a lesser extent, to those in neighbouring quadrants. It is the people in the quadrant opposite yours that provide you with the toughest challenges. For example, if yours is a socialite character then your instinct will be to sell with enthusiasm. That is just the quality most likely to repel an analyser character.

Of course, the answer is that when you understand another person's character you can adapt your sales style to suit them. Once you are comfortable with this method, and are able to adapt your style appropriately, you will find a considerable improvement in how you relate to and persuade other people. The uses of this knowledge extend far beyond selling.

So why do people so often misjudge others?

There are six key reasons for doing so, and the first three are closely related.

1 Stereotyping

The best-known reason. It describes our tendency to group together people with similar characteristics and allocate traits to them on the basis of that grouping. When selling, you will find that some stereotypes have some basis in fact. For example, finance directors tend to be more focused on profit; sales directors more on turnover. Of course, the danger is that you focus on the stereotype and miss the key characteristics of the individual that would help you make the sale.

2 Being misled by a significant characteristic you notice early on

Psychologists term this the 'halo effect'. What it means is that a particular and striking feature of a person can colour all that we subsequently learn about them. For example, at a job interview the candidate dressed immaculately will start off with a positive halo effect and the interviewer's image of them will be distorted from then on.

Salespeople frequently fall into this trap because the first thing they notice about the prospect is often a distraction. The effect is enhanced by the fact that we are more likely to notice characteristics we share with the other person and we are more likely to overrate those shared characteristics. 'Halos' can be positive or negative features. The point about them is that they distort your subsequent vision.

3 Making what psychologists term a 'logical error'

If we believe an individual has a particular trait we often assume they will have related traits. For example, when we notice that someone is plump we tend subconsciously to assume that they are happier than average. (Whereas research suggests that plump people are only averagely happy.)

In 1950 Professor H. H. Kelley set up a now famous experiment to test the strength of this effect. He invited a colleague to lecture to his psychology students for 20 minutes before engaging those students in conversation. Prior to the lecture he split his students into two groups and described the lecturer as 'warm' to one group and 'cold' to the other. When the lecture had finished and the colleague had left the room, Professor Kelley asked the students to write their descriptions of him. The students who were told that he was going to be 'cold' were much more likely to use words such as self-centred, unsociable, humourless and ruthless in their descriptions than the students who were told he was 'warm'. On top of that, the students who had been told the lecturer was 'warm' were more likely to interact with him in the discussion: 56 per cent did as opposed to 32 per cent of the other group.

What happened here was that one falsely perceived trait led many of the students to gain a totally altered view of the guest lecturer. Most of us have fallen for this trap many times in our lives. You need to watch out for it when selling.

4 Seeing what we are motivated to see

We are much more likely to notice things when they relate to our present needs and objectives. A thirsty person will notice a glass of water. Mark Twain summed up this very human trait when he wrote that 'He who has a hammer sees everything as a nail'. Salespeople often misinterpret the words and gestures of prospects as buying signals and so misinterpret their chances of winning deals. (On average, they misinterpret things by 25–30 per cent as we shall see in Chapter 15, on measuring sales performance.)

5 Seeing what we expect to see

To a large extent we see what we expect to see. For example, researchers conducted an experiment to test whether teachers' beliefs about particular students influenced the marks attained by those students. The test was to submit the work of students of whom teachers had high expectations under the names of students of whom the teachers had low expectations. It led to consistently lower marks being awarded to the less favoured students. When the test was reversed, the same degree of teacher influence could be seen. The lesson here is to approach things with an open mind.

6 Judging the other person's mood rather than their character

If you first meet someone on what was for them a bad day you will probably have a worse opinion of them than had you met them on a good day. Just as storm clouds can blight a pleasant landscape, so the sun brightens a dull one.

All told, being objective about other people is very difficult, but with the two-scale method described in this chapter you will be better able to do that better than most. But so much for judging the character of others. Now it is time to look at the strongest of all forces in selling ...

Chapter **3**

Using emotion in selling

- Honesty
- Charm
- Using emotion correctly
- The emotions behind buying decisions

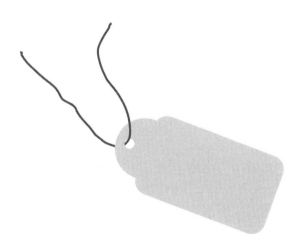

'Mankind are governed more by their feelings than by reason.'

Samuel Adams (1722–1803) American patriot and politician

In selling, as in so much of life, a high emotional intelligence can be more useful to you than a high IQ. That is what this chapter is about.

People buy from people they like

Being personable is a huge advantage in selling. People don't buy from companies, they buy from people. That means that whenever they can they will buy from someone they like and trust.

In nearly all sales it is emotion, not logic, that persuades people to buy. (What usually happens is that people buy on emotional grounds and then justify their decision on logical grounds.) Logic on its own has very little persuasive power. You should speak more to the heart than the head. The only real exception to this rule occurs when people buy commodities.

You need to act honestly

The best successes occur when you build lasting relationships with customers who grow to trust and rely on you. It is one reason why the best salespeople do not come across as salespeople.

FIGURE 1

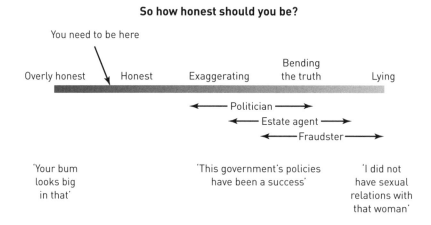

So how honest should you be?

You may well have met people who sell towards the right-hand side of this spectrum and you probably didn't like them. So why do they sell like that? Well, a few of them would have done it because they lacked a conscience. (Psychologists believe this condition affects about 1 per cent of the general population.) However, the overwhelming majority would have done so to defer awkward problems until a later date. It is a very human trap to fall into – and one you need to avoid.

So how do you create charm?

As with so many things, Shakespeare summed up the essence of charm better than anyone before or since. He said that charm most frequently occurs when a person is 'kind and courteous' in equal measure. Nowadays we might express that as when integrity and savoir-faire are equally balanced in a person's character. Too much integrity makes us seem blunt; too much savoir-faire makes us seem slippery. People with both qualities equally balanced, and present in reasonable quantities, are the ones best able to charm. But how should they do it?

Focus the emotion in the right area

Sales conversations fall into one of three types. These are:

> **Personal/personal conversations:** These conversations just focus on personal issues and have nothing to do with business. They are conversations about the news, recent sports events, the weather and such like. In business, this type of conversation often happens when you first meet someone and there is a place for it at that point. It will not however, go far to increasing your sales.

> **Business/business conversations:** These conversations are the exact opposite. They are essentially impersonal conversations about business issues. They are conversations along the lines of: 'So Mr Customer, how would this proposed development affect the company?'

> **Business/personal conversations:** These conversations sound at first glance to be similar to business/business conversations but there is a subtle difference. Usually, they take one of two slightly different forms. The first form asks how your prospect *feels* about something. For example: 'So Mr Customer, how do *feel* this proposed development will affect the company?' The second form is slightly stronger. It asks how something will *affect them personally*. Typically, it will be a question such as: 'So, Mr Customer, how will the proposed development affect your own situation here?' In both cases the question is directed at the emotions the prospect feels about his business world.

The key to using emotion in selling is to focus on the business/personal. It will aid the consultative approach and will help you gain trust. The prospect will see you not just as 'another consultant' but as someone who is 'focused on them'. They may well perceive this subconsciously, but they will perceive it.

Business/personal conversations are also more likely to uncover real buying motives. In contrast, a business/business approach is more likely to get a 'standard' response.

One final note. Avoid the trap of asking, 'How does *the company* feel about this?' Instead, say 'How do *you* feel about this?' Asking how the company feels about things will get you the standard response.

What are the emotions behind buying decisions?

The rational part of the buyer will think about the reasons for buying but at the same time emotion will flow over those thoughts. We already know that people buy on emotional grounds and then justify their decision on logical grounds. What we should also know is that those emotions are capable of very powerful effects. But exactly which emotions are at work here?

There is of course a wide sea of emotions, but by far the most powerful, from the point of view of selling, are fear and greed. They can be so powerful as to leave rationality bobbing like a cork upon them. (It is for this reason that Benjamin Franklin's decision-making method was such a good idea.)

Yet, despite their power, you should never use fear or greed to sell. If you try, the prospect will see what you are doing and dislike you for it. What you must do, however, is be respectful of these two emotions because they are usually present and they are usually powerful. That way, you will have some empathy with your prospect.

Fear of loss and desire for gain

But which emotion, fear or greed, is the more powerful? In reality they are two sides of the same coin. Most people fear loss more than they desire gain. If you give a group of people a 50:50 chance, for example a chance to gain £2,000 or to lose £2,000, most of the group will choose not to play. They fear the loss more than they desire the gain. Shakespeare also summed up this emotion rather well. He wrote that: 'Things of like value, but differing in their owners, are prized by their masters.' What this means is we tend to value something we already own more than something we could own. It is a type of inertia.

Scientists have been able to put a figure on the strength of this emotion, thanks to research undertaken by Richard Thaler, Daniel Kahneman and Jack Knetsch at Cornell University, New York in 1990. To gauge that strength they first gave one set of students coffee mugs emblazoned with the Cornell motif. The students were allowed to take the mugs home with them. A few weeks later, they were asked for the lowest price at which they would sell their mug. The average price they gave was $5.25. A second set of students were shown the mugs and asked the top price they would pay to own one. The average answer was $2.25. As we saw in Chapter 1, people generally think that a reasonable price is 40–50 per cent of your first quote. It so happens that $2.25 is 43 per cent of $5.25.

So far, we have just looked at how emotion affects the buyer. But can the seller use their own emotions to help with the selling? The answer, perhaps surprisingly, is not that much. True, emotion can help with certain parts of selling. In negotiation, for instance (Chapter 18), or motivation (Chapter 20), or in the enthusiasm you show when selling to a socialite. But showing emotion per se is of little use. For example, most people value the financial advice of a staid bank manager over that of an exuberant free thinker, even when both of those people give the same advice. The reason is that the bank manager appears the safer option of the two. A conservative image is usually a safe bet when selling.

There is, however, one area of emotion that is tremendously useful for the seller:

Intuition

Nowadays we are conditioned to believe that information uncovered by science is of better quality than information uncovered by our own senses. But is that really true? Your senses are the result of several million years' testing in a harsh environment. By contrast there is a close association between things labelled 'new technology' and things that do not work.

Most people have strong intuition – if they would but use it.

But of course, emotion is not just about what you say. It is about how you appear, too ...

Chapter **4**

Body language in sales meetings

- The importance of body language in selling
- Persuasive and non-persuasive body language
- What to look for in others

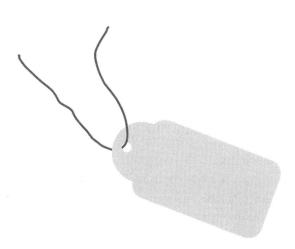

'The city is not a concrete jungle, it is a human zoo.'
Desmond Morris (b. 1928), body language expert

Where body language is concerned, you probably know a lot more than you think you do. Therefore this chapter just focuses on the more subtle parts of the subject that you may not know about, and on the parts that are specifically related to sales. In the past you might have half guessed at what these signs and signals mean, but knowing their literal meaning will complement that intuition.

How important is body language in sales?

The UCLA psychologist and researcher Albert Mehrabian was the pioneer of modern research into this subject. His conclusions, arrived at in the mid-1970s, were that in face-to-face meetings communication is made up of the following:

> spoken words: 7 per cent
> intonation: 38 per cent
> body language: 55 per cent.

Collectively we tend to overrate the value of verbal language in communication. This is probably because language can communicate complex and abstract ideas in a way that no other method can. However, most of what we communicate is neither complex nor abstract but concerned with basic emotions. And these basic emotions are often communicated most clearly by body language. Several studies have found that when a listener feels there is a conflict between a person's words and their body language, the listener is more likely to believe the body language.

Persuasive and non-persuasive body language

Body language in sales falls into two categories. Body language from you that either persuades or dissuades the prospect; and the body language you observe in others. Let us look first at body language that persuades and dissuades.

Persuasive body language

> **Nodding your head when the prospect speaks:** This is easy to do, and puts you at a tremendous advantage. Most people feel that

salespeople do not listen enough, and nodding your head is a very good way to dispel such feelings.

➤ **Mirroring:** Mirroring means that you subtly copy the stance of your prospect (Fig. 1). We naturally do this with people we like, and when others mirror us we feel in harmony with that person. Good mirroring does not just mean adopting the same stance. Your blinking and breathing should also match the other person. When you do that, the effect of mirroring becomes very powerful.

FIGURE 1

Mirroring

Non-persuasive body language

➤ **Putting up barriers:** It is best to avoid a wide cross of the legs because this puts a barrier between you and your prospect (Fig. 2). For similar reasons you should keep your arms open at all times. Crossed arms imply a barrier and they can suggest you are hiding something.

FIGURE 2

Wide cross

FIGURE 3A

Mirroring

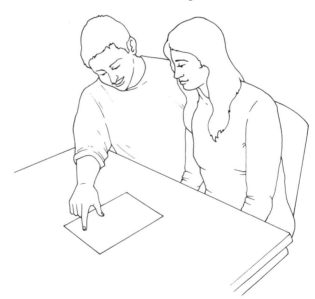

Sitting confrontationally

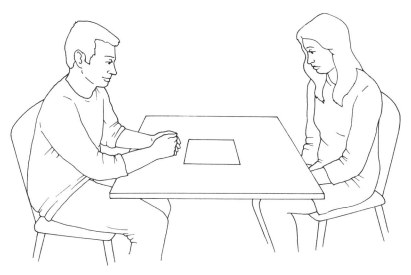

> **Sitting inappropriately:** You should never lean back in the presence of your prospect. It will make you appear either aloof or lazy. The best posture is to lean very slightly forward, as that shows interest in the prospect. Just avoid leaning too far forward as that communicates pushiness. If you can, avoid sitting opposite your prospect (Fig. 3B). Sitting at the side of the desk is a lot less confrontational (Fig. 3A).

Body language to observe in others

Body language will not just improve the way others see you. It will help you see what others are thinking. Here are some signs to look out for when selling.

Barriers

If your prospect has crossed arms it usually means they want more of a barrier between you. (They might want this consciously or subconsciously.) A common reason for creating this barrier is that they do not fully believe what you have just said. If that is the reason then it will always be a genuine objection, never a false one – and you will need to overcome it before you can carry the conversation forward.

There are, of course, several variations on this theme of crossed arms. A person holding a cufflink is often a type of barrier. So is holding a cup with both hands.

Interested evaluation

A common expression of interested evaluation is the hand on the cheek. Usually this is signalled by a person's thumb and first finger pointing upwards, and the other three fingers curled. Similarly, people tend to tilt their head to one side when a subject interests them.

FIGURE 4

Interested evaluation is the sign that usually precedes the steepled hands of decision-making.

The eyes have it

As people move from evaluation to interest, your attention should move to their eyes. The eyes have a language of their own that can give us away and reveal our innermost thoughts, showing both the songs and the sorrows of our souls. However, your intuition can interpret the language in a prospect's eyes far better than any book. What this book can do is describe two particular aspects of a prospect's eyes that you should pay attention to when selling:

- > People blink more frequently when they are interested in what you have to offer. That is a buying signal.
- > A person's pupils will dilate when they want something. It is another buying signal and one that cannot be faked. (It is one of the reasons why poker players wear dark glasses.) Research by Eckhard Hess of the University of Chicago in the mid-1970s quantified the degree to which this happens, and his research suggests the effect is significant. Essentially our pupils dilate when we see something we desire and contract when we see something we dislike.

Gazing

Research conducted at American universities suggests that, in western culture, the most successful business meetings are those in which the parties make direct eye-to-eye contact for approximately one-third of the time. In meetings with less eye contact than this participants reported feelings of a lack of rapport with the other person. In the meetings with more than one-third eye contact the meetings were often described as too confrontational and overly personal.

Where to gaze Research also shows that it matters where on your prospect's face you focus your gaze. The best rapport is gained when you focus on the area from the middle of the forehead to the upper lip. Gazing below this line is too personal. Gazing above is too aloof.

Avoiding gazes We often distrust those who won't look at us and we avoid an interaction by avoiding eye contact. If the prospect is avoiding your gaze it usually means they have mentally ruled you out of the sale and are just going through the motions of seeing suppliers.

Gaze patterns and status Gaze patterns are very accurate measures of status because a person who feels dominant will gaze much less than a person who is trying to establish dominance. The probable reason for this is that the higher the status of the individual the less they feel they need to observe the behaviour of subordinates. The special factor to be aware of here is gender. Research by the Californian Professor Nancy Henley, a world specialist on this, shows that women in high-status positions tend to gaze much more at subordinates than do men in equivalent high-status positions.

Smiling

So how do you know if a smile is genuine or faked? You probably find it easy to spot fake smiles when looking through old family photos, but why exactly can you do that? Well, a genuine smile is characterised by five things:

> it appears symmetrical
> it lasts for what seems a 'correct' length of time
> it has crows' feet at the side of the eyes
> it includes a lowering of the brows
> it forms bags under the eyes.

If you now try to do those five things together while looking delighted you will see why a genuine smile is so hard to fake. Even the best actors have trouble.

How can you tell if someone is lying?

People try many ways to mask a lie but your intuition will probably warn you if the prospect is not being honest. You can check your intuition by looking for six signals. Most people can fake one or two of the signals, but faking all six at the same time is remarkably difficult.

> **The eyes:** A liar's eyes look away and down more than a truth teller's.
> **The hands:** A liar's hands move much less than a truth teller's.
> **Focus on self:** When people lie they talk much more about themselves than they do when telling the truth. The reason they do this is that liars find it is easier to rely on their own 'evidence' than on other peoples' when lying. Excessive use of 'I' or 'me' in conversation should alert you to this possibility.
> **Fleeting expressions:** These are the expressions that appear on a liar's face for an instant before they are 'corrected'. They are an excellent way of seeing what a person is really feeling.
> **Self-touching:** Most children will cover their mouths the moment after they lie, but as we get older, we learn to disguise this response. When an adult lies the hand will still move towards the mouth but is usually diverted before it gets there – typically to the eye, ear or neck.
> **Leg and foot actions:** People tend to fidget more when they lie. Skilled liars suppress the fidgeting of their hands and upper body, but they will not be so good at suppressing the fidgeting in their

legs and feet. For this reason the movements of legs and feet are often good indicators of the truth.

Handshakes

A word about handshakes:

> **The dominating handshake:** This is a handshake in which one person puts their hand above the other person's hand, rather than to the side of it. You should always avoid doing this. If you think of the people who shake your hand this way you will probably find you do not like any of them.

FIGURE 5

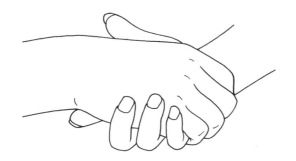

> **The reinforced handshake:** This is where the left hand reinforces the right in some way. You most commonly see politicians using this type of handshake – a strong indication that it is an insincere way to shake hands.

FIGURE 6

The final thing to remember when shaking hands is to look the other person in the eye. (Most people look at the hands instead.)

So much for meetings. Some of them will end with you being required to submit a proposal ...

Chapter **5**

How to write proposals

- The best way to write a proposal
- Management summary
- Introduction
- Your understanding of their requirements
- Your company's suitability for the work
- The proposed way forward
- Costs
- Possible next steps

'That which is written without effort is usually read without pleasure.'

Samuel Johnson (1709–84), writer

Written proposals need two things – good structure and good English. This chapter is about the structure. (The next one is about good English.) Structure is important for writing. It is the reason why the people who write plays are called 'playwrights,' rather than 'playwrites'. Plays are only good when they are well constructed, and the same goes for anything you write.

A sales proposal will only have a clear structure when the writer has clarity of thought. An excellent way to gain this clarity of thought is by constructing your proposals in four stages. Most people find this technique improves the quality of their writing significantly. Here is how you do it.

> **Stage 1, Structure:** The first stage is a written plan that describes the structure of the proposal. It has much the same role to the proposal as a skeleton has to a body.
>
>   This stage 1 describes the order of the chapter headings and the contents of the chapter sub-headings. If the proposal is less than two pages it will also specify the subject of each paragraph. An example of this stage 1 is given on page 55.

> **Stage 2, Words:** Stage 2 is your first draft of the finished article. As soon as you have written it, it needs reviewing by a colleague.

> **Stage 3, Final format:** This stage starts with the correction of the errors highlighted by that colleague review. There will usually be a lot. Once you have made those corrections you should prepare another 'finished article' and submit that for review. (You can be sure that will throw up yet more faults.)

> **Stage 4, Ready to send:** This is the final check of the final version. Once it is done, your document can be sent out.

So why do it that way? The process is disarmingly simple, but it has four advantages:

> **It gives order, and clarity of thought.** The biggest weakness of most sales documents is that they are not thought through fully at the beginning. That is like building a house without an architect's drawings. Stage 1 forces you to think through your document – and that helps ensure good structure.

> **It creates a better end product.** People who regularly read proposals will tell you that nearly all of them have typographical errors and poor style. The second and third stages reduce these problems significantly.

> **It is the quickest and most practical way to do it.** Tender documents arriving at your office usually come with short

timeframes for your response. This process will help you meet those timeframes because it brings order to the bid-writing process and allows you to set target dates for completing each stage.

> **It is something you have to do at some time.** You simply cannot write a good quality document without putting effort into the structure. You can put off doing this part of the job, but that just makes for more work in the end. The best time to sort the structure is at the beginning.

What should be in a proposal?

At first glance the requests for proposals arriving at your office will seem very different. However, when you look at what they are actually requesting they turn out to be very similar. This means that:

> your replies will be very similar

> it makes sense to invest time in producing a good template for those replies.

To follow is just such a template, built in sections. The purpose of each section is described and there are notes that form a stage 1 for each section. The template will work for about 90 per cent of the proposals you will ever write, and you are welcome to download it from www.secrets-of-selling.com for your own use. (Readers who sell products might feel this template has a bias towards services, but actually it works for selling both products and services. The reason is that when you are selling large amounts of a product the dynamics of the sale change. The more that is sold the less the buyer is concerned about trust in the product and the more they are concerned about trust in your company.)

Section 1: Management summary

This section is written very much from a business perspective. Therefore it is usually best written by people whose skills lie more in the selling than the technical side of your profession. It may well be the only part the senior executive reads, so it needs to encapsulate the key benefits of your proposal.

Also, the management summary is the only part of the proposal that does not fit into the four-stage construction process. Although it is the

FIGURE 1

Cover page

Prospect's logo

Project name

Your company logo

Date

Prepared for:	**Prepared by:**
Prospect's details	Your company's details

Reference number
Reviewed by

Table of contents

1 Management summary
2 Introduction
3 Our understanding of your requirements
4 Our suitability for the work
5 The proposed way forward
   5.1 Understanding the key issues
   5.2 Examining the possibilities
   5.3 Making recommendations
6 Costs
   6.1 Our method of billing
   6.2 Breakdown of the costs
7 Possible next steps

---

first thing to appear in the finished document it should be the last part you actually write because that is the time when you will be able to make the best of it. It is a module in its own right.

Stage 1 of the management summary

> Summarise the client's situation.

> Summarise what you are proposing to do.

> Summarise how you will do the work. If possible, condense this into four or five bullet points.

> Summarise why you would be a good company to do the work, and the benefits the prospect would receive. Condense this into bullet points too.

> Then summarise the financial aspects of your proposal.

Section 2: Introduction

This should be a short section, rarely more than a paragraph. It should summarise the dates of the meetings you had with the prospect that led to the creation of the proposal and should also list the people who attended those meetings. The introduction should not include the contents of those meetings. That is best left to the next section.

The real purpose of the introduction is to set the scene and show that you keep good records. It also allows you to sweep some of the messy but necessary parts of your proposal into one neat section.

Stage 1 of the introduction

> You need to give the dates of previous meetings, and who attended them, that led to this proposal being written.

> If your proposal is a response to a request for a proposal (RFP) then this is the place to mention it.

Section 3: Your understanding of their requirements

We already know that much of selling is about demonstrating an under-standing of and meeting requirements. Therefore the key purpose of this section is to show the prospect that you have a thorough and complete understanding of their situation. The quality of this section will be directly proportional to the quality of the notes you took at the meeting.

Stage 1 of understanding their requirements

> Write an overview of the prospect's company and its business situation.

> Position the technical situation.

➤ Position the particular issues.

➤ Describe the benefits to be gained from resolving these issues successfully.

Section 4: Your company's suitability for the work

This section should highlight the reasons why your company is well suited to the work. Your instinct may well be to list a large number of reasons here, but that is rarely your best course. You will be much more persuasive if you just list the top three or four reasons. This apparent contradiction works because of a curious aspect of human behaviour – namely that the fewer fact-based reasons people have for supporting a particular view, the more powerful their emotion-based reasons become for that support.

Stage 1 of your company's suitability for the work

➤ Say you are keen to do the work and believe there are a number of reasons why your company is suited to it.

➤ Then list those reasons with credentials to back them up.

Section 5: The proposed way forward

This section describes how your company will do the work. Depending on the circumstances of the proposal you may well want to describe a small piece of work, or a first delivery date, that your company could do as a lead-in to the main piece. As was mentioned in Chapter 1, it is easier, psychologically, for the prospect to agree to a small deal to get things going – and that is all you need to win. If the decision is being made by a group rather than an individual the effect will be magnified, because a 'no further commitments' lead-in piece of work is exactly the type of compromise that appeals to committees.

Stage 1 of the proposed way forward

➤ Say how you are going to start. If you are selling a service, this will almost certainly be by talking to the people closest to the issues, so write a few lines describing how you will do that.

➤ After that you will probably look at what is technically possible, so write a few lines describing your process for doing that.

➤ Then you are probably going to think about recommendations before presenting them to the client, so you should describe that process too.

Section 6: Costs

You should explain your approach to billing in a clear and open way. With services this means including a summary of your day rates, your expenses and any one-off charges. With products it means a clear definition of delivery and billing dates.

Clarity, not ambiguity, is your best friend when you write this part of the proposal because issues that are avoided now will tend to rebound on you later – and when that happens they could damage the trust between you and the prospect. Trust is a very important factor when selling and it needs nurturing at every stage of the sales process. Being scrupulously open about your costs is a good way to gain trust, and it is unlikely that all your competitors will be as open as you are. Imagine a situation where you have detailed all the extra costs, such as expenses, equipment hire, VAT, etc., and your competitor has not. In the eyes of the prospect, you will look the more honest partner.

Stage 1 of the costs

> ➤ You need to say whether your proposal is fixed price or time and materials (more about this in Chapter 19). If it is time and materials you should say how accurate you think your estimates are. This is best described by giving a likely variance of plus or minus per cent. For example, 'These costs are accurate to a variance of +/– 10 per cent'. You should also summarise the methodologies you have used to make predictions and you should explain your expenses policy.

> ➤ You need to break down the costs so they are clear and simple – much like the following table.

FIGURE 2

Summarising your costs clearly

Task	Days spent by consultant		Cost
	£1,000 per day rate	£400 per day rate	
Project design	0.25	0.5	£450
Implementation		3	£1,200
Testing		1	£400
Project management	0.5		£500
Total			**£2,550**

Section 7: Possible next steps

In Chapter 1, we looked at the reasons why a salesperson should *actually* ask for the work. Of course your proposal cannot quite ask for the work in the way a human can, but what you should do in this section is refer again to the small piece of work that will get things started.

Stage 1 of the possible next steps

➤ Summarise the 'lead-in' piece of work or first delivery and invite the prospect to accept your offer.

➤ You may want to put a time limit on the validity of your quote.

The final thing to say about proposals is:

Keep all your past proposals in one place

New proposals often contain material from old proposals. Therefore you will save a lot of time if you keep all your old proposals in a place that is accessible to everyone in your company (something that does not happen in many companies).

This central store of old proposals should not just contain the proposals. With each proposal there should be a summary document that contains:

➤ a technical overview of each piece of work

➤ a description of the business application of the work

➤ an outline of the benefits to the client.

Of course the danger to avoid with all this is to be drawn into boilerplate responses – responses that are not tailored to the requirement.

Now that you have the structure of your document, it is time to look at the words you will hang from that structure ...

Chapter **6**

Writing words that sell

- The rules for writing good English
- How to write case studies
- How to write one-page summaries

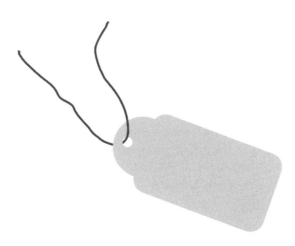

'I do not so much dislike the matter, but the manner of his speech.'

William Shakespeare (1564–1616), poet and playwright

The Economist is an unusually well-written magazine. It describes the holy trinity of journalism as articles that are 'factually correct, well thought-out and elegantly expressed'. That's exactly how your sales documents should be written. The need to get things 'factually correct' has been mentioned several times, and the last chapter showed the method for producing a 'well thought-out' proposal. This chapter is about 'elegant expression'. Most proposals are not elegantly expressed – and that is a chance for you to shine.

How do you write good English?

Actually, it is very simple. The writer George Orwell summarised six rules that describe how anyone can do it. They are:

1 Never use a metaphor, simile or other figure of speech which you are used to seeing in print.

2 Never use a long word where a short word will do.

3 If it is possible to cut a word out, always cut it out.

4 Never use the passive when you can use the active.

5 Never use a foreign phrase, a scientific word or a jargon word if you can think of an everyday English equivalent.

6 Break any of these rules sooner than say anything barbarous.

Let us look more closely at each of these.

Never use a metaphor, simile or other figure of speech which you are used to seeing in print

Similes and metaphors compare things. The difference is that while a simile just suggests two things are similar, a metaphor suggests they are as one. So 'the world is like a stage' is a simile; 'the world's a stage' is a metaphor.

You should avoid tired metaphors and similes until the cows are blue in the face. They will add nothing to your writing.

Never use a long word when a short word will do

This is because short words are easier to understand. The most practical way to do this in real life is to prefer words that have their root in English over words that have their root in Latin. There are two other advantages to using English-based words:

> English-based words are usually clearer, so your reader is more likely to understand what you mean the first time round. People are so busy nowadays that they will not thank you for having to read a document twice.

> People who use English-based words are seen as more trustworthy than those who use Latin-based words. Researchers tested this by analysing the speech patterns of a variety of professions. They found that the two groups of people who used Latin-based words more than anyone else in society were politicians and estate agents. That surely proves trustworthiness beyond any reasonable doubt. (Lawyers came third.) There was however, one notable exception to this rule. When the speeches of politicians were analysed one politician stood out as using a much lower percentage of Latin-based words than any other: Winston Churchill. 'We shall fight them on the beaches' for example, is composed only of English-based words. As he pointed out himself, with Latin-based words it becomes: 'Hostilities will be engaged with our adversary along the coastal perimeter'.

If it is possible to cut a word out, always cut it out

US President Abraham Lincoln was once asked to deliver a speech and was asked how long he would need to prepare. He replied,

It depends on how long you want me to speak. If you want me to speak for five minutes it will take me two weeks to prepare. If you want me to speak for an hour it will take me a week to prepare. If you want me to talk all day, I am ready now.

Distilling your words takes time but means

> your writing is easier to understand

> it is more likely to be read – people prefer short documents

> it is harder for the competition to rebut your arguments. When faced with two points of view people tend to prefer the simpler one.

When first you write a sentence, it is difficult to distil it fully. If you use the four-stage process for writing documents you will have several chances to distil the meaning you want to convey and so improve the end document.

FIGURE 1

The word distillery

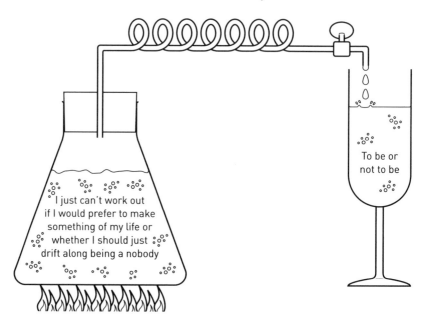

However, you should not apply this rule absolutely because a little padding can make your words easier to understand. An analogy can be made with the human body. You do not need an array of body-mass index charts and fat-pinching callipers to know whether someone is the right weight. You know that just by looking at them. The truth is the human body looks best when it has just a little fat on it and the same applies to writing. A little padding makes it easier on the eye, but you only ever want a little.

Never use the passive when you can use the active

Using the active tense injects energy into your writing and that helps to keep the reader's attention. For example 'She's pointing a gun at you' is a lot more compelling than 'A gun was pointed at you'.

Never use a foreign phrase, a scientific word or a jargon word if you can think of an everyday English equivalent

These words tend to alienate ordinary readers. It is easy to make things sound complicated but the best salespeople are those who can translate the technical jargon of their work into language that their clients can easily understand.

The chances are your competitors write proposals that are incontinent with jargon, with phrases such as 'The purpose of our company is to empower its clients with holistic business solutions'. Such phrases say more about the writer than they do about the company.

So why do people write like that? Well, the reasons are psychological, and the top three reasons are:

> egotism

> a perceived need to construct defences

> thinking too little about the reader.

These people are betrayed by their words. Would you buy from someone whose writing suggests them to be egotistic, defensive and inward-focused?

Whenever you write a document you should run it past Orwell's six rules. However, when writing sales proposals you need to apply an extra three rules.

Liven it up

Your proposals will have far more impact if they incorporate colour and the prospect company's logo. Within reason you should put in graphs and charts. All these things make your documents more readable and they make you look more professional.

Write in a modern style

A common style mistake in business is to write in outdated language. It is the written equivalent of putting on a telephone voice. The property descriptions of real-estate agents are classic examples of this.

A related point is the use of 'company fonts'. Some companies use them to add individuality, which on its own is a good thing. However, some fonts are unfamiliar to the eye and they slow down reading significantly. Research suggests this can be by as much as 50 per cent.

Involve your prospect in the bid-writing process

The point here is that most prospects will be pleased to tell you exactly what they would like to see written in your proposal and you can capitalise on that. Here is how.

Early on in the bid process you should try and arrange to meet with the prospect on a date that is two or three days before the proposal is due in. The purpose of the meeting is for you and the prospect to review your draft proposal – your stage 4 – prior to you formally submitting it. Most prospects will agree to this and the process will have two positive benefits for you:

> The prospect will naturally pick up on any parts of the proposal that conflict with what they want to see and they will tell you what changes they want to see. You then make those changes before the formal submission.

> When you submit the final proposal it will be, in effect, as though the prospect has all but written it themselves. The prospect is more likely to accept such a proposal.

A prospect will not think less of you for making such a suggestion because it shows you want to listen to their needs. The worst they will say is that they cannot allow you an 'unfair' advantage over the competition.

Proofreading

Spell-checkers will allow you to send a daft contract instead of a draft contract. When my wife worked for one of the large consulting firms she once typed a 120-page summary of the flotation plans for a major football club entitled 'Going pubic'.

When such mistakes are made with prices the courts will sometimes enforce the mistake. For example, a well-known aircraft maker lost a court case in which it stated that the omission of a zero from a price it quoted in a proposal was a typing error. It probably was, but the judge ruled that the planes be sold at the reduced price.

The most common proofreading mistakes are:

> Accepting what the spell-checker and grammar checker tell you. (The grammar checker in particular is often wrong.)

> Punctuation mistakes.

> Not being consistent with the spaces after full stops. You can have either one or two spaces after a full stop, but you must be consistent.

When you are getting your documents proofread, try to make sure that at least one of those proofreaders has never seen the document before.

What sales documents will you need?

The world is full of glossy brochures about companies and products. Many have pictures of people crowded round a laptop and that text about 'holistic business solutions'. Brochures like that add very little to the sales process. The only sales documents you really need when visiting a prospect are:

> case studies of your past work
> a one-page summary of your company's products and services.

Anything more is usually superfluous, and could be counterproductive.

Imagine the scene. A salesperson has been listening to a prospect for an hour and it is time for the meeting to end. In the closing remarks the salesperson says something like, 'Here is a brochure we have on that; I'll be in contact next week to see if we can do this work for you'.

You have probably witnessed many such scenes and this example is just one of the ways in which glossy brochures can impede selling. Just as people typically take in little of what we say, they typically take in little of what they read in glossy brochures. Therefore you are better off with a small amount of good material than a large amount of something more average.

So what should be in a case study?

Case studies say, in essence, that you have done similar work before and you did that work well. They are one of the most potent weapons in your armoury. You will rarely have enough of them so you should do what you can to alleviate the shortage. This means getting your client's permission to write up their project as a case study, and the best time to do that is when the project is being signed off. That is when they are most likely to agree to such a request.

Here is an example case study, written first as a stage 1, and then as a stage 4:

FIGURE 2

Case study, stage 1

Client name and project name
Put a one-sentence summary of the work here, including the primary benefit
One-paragraph summary of the work
Summary of the client's commercial situation
Summary of the client's technical situation
Summary of what was done, including what your company did
Summary of how this benefited the client
Footer should describe your company in two sentences and put in contact details

FIGURE 3

Case study, stage 4

Goverment audit
Background
Holistic Paradigms Consulting first worked for the UK Department of Transport on a project to improve efficiency. The outcomes of this project, such as the initiative to improve typing speeds across the Department, were well received. The success of the relationship meant that Holistic Paradigms was a natural choice when a particular project at the Department's West London offices needed auditing.

Issues
The original specification of the project has required repair of the office air conditioning. However, cost overruns meant the work has involved shifting 6.5 million cubic metres (230 million cubic feet) of earth which relandscaped 260 hectares (640 acres) of West London and cost £4.2 billion to complete.

Solution
The Department felt that a consultancy was needed to learn lessons from this and so turned to Holistic Paradigms.

Holistic Paradigms' input
Holistic Paradigms examined internal departmental documents and the actual contract between the Department and the suppliers. This showed the original requirement was for 'a new airpump to ease congestion in the air conditioning' but the tender document had in fact asked for 'a new airport to ease congestion in the air conditions', the error being caused by the increased typing speeds employed by the Department.

Holistic Paradigms were also able to ascertain that a new terminal and runway had been built next to the Department's Heathrow office.

Benefits to the client
The Department was able to participate in the project by choosing a name for the new aiport of Project/TendersAirCon/para 3.1/typoerror until a further typing error caused it to be renamed Heathrow Terminal 5.

One-page summaries and how to write them

A one-page summary is a succinct description of what your company or your product does. It is essentially a written version of the thumbnail sketch and will probably be the most useful sales document you possess.

This book cannot provide a universal template for one-page summaries because companies are so different. However, the following three examples do cover most eventualities. The first example is a stage 1 for an IT services company. The second is a stage 4 for a legal practice. The third is a stage 4 for an IT product.

The essential difference between the two companies used in these examples is this: a key sales issue for IT companies is proving the business value of their work, whereas a key sales issue for legal practices is making themselves appear different from their competitors.

FIGURE 4

One-page summary of an IT services company, stage 1

Introduction
This should be two or three sentences that summarise what your company does and why that is useful. This section should capture the concentrated essence of your company.

Experience
This summarises the industry sectors in which you have worked.

Applications
This summarises the business applications of your work and the benefits that flow from those applications.

Your specialist area of expertise
You need to write this part so that both an ordinary reader, and someone from the same profession as you, would draw meaning from it.

Clients
References are more powerful when the client is well known, so choose blue-chip names whenever you can.

Locations
Be aware of the value clients place on their suppliers being close by. Location is particularly important for service companies.

FIGURE 5

One-page summary of a legal services company, stage 4

Wells, Preece and Rogers   *85% success rate in*
business-to-business
litigation

Wellers, Preece and Rogers is a specialist law firm. We specialise in just five areas of the law:

- Business leases
- Commercial intellectual property rights
- Corporate responsibility
- Business contracts
- Commercial litigation

So what makes us different from other law firms?
From the inception of our company we have focused on these five areas and have now gained a market-leading position in them.

There is nothing stuffy or academic about our practice. The company is geared to providing clients with advice that is human, pragmatic and commercial. To this end the company is composed of specialist teams that each have a specific focus on a specific sector. This ensures our staff are not just legal experts in a given field but also have a close understanding of your business. We invest heavily in staff development to ensure our staff remain leaders in their fields, so further benefiting our clients.

The company is focused on building long-term relationships with our clients and if we make a mistake we will stick with the client until we get it right. For these reasons we have very high levels of repeat business.

The company includes 29 partners and 145 legally qualified staff.

Different services to meet different needs
We go the extra mile to make ourselves accessible to our clients. For example, many clients benefit from our 'lawyer on call' service which allows unlimited access to a dedicated legal team for a set quarterly fee. The clients are able to discuss their day-to-day legal needs without one eye on the clock. This nips many legal issues in the bud – before they grow into problems – and it allows our staff to gain a detailed understanding of your business. So allowing us to further help you.

Contact us at:

Wellers, Preece and Rogers: *'What do you want today?'*

FIGURE 6

One-page summary for a product

ER●S.
Enterprise Risk & Opportunity System

Business overview
EROS is the first completely web-based risk and opportunity system. It enables corporations and individuals to effectively and proactively manage risks and opportunities.

Today's organisations tend to manage risk on an ad hoc basis, learning few lessons. **EROS** allows users to apply a structured risk management culture throughout an organisation. The product is proactive and intuitive. It has a web-based nature that allows for the extensive use of e-mail and browsers.

Key benefits:
- Instils a consistent and holistic approach to risk management throughout an organisation, across all departments and geographic locations.
- Gives you dynamic and up-to-date information at the push of a button, allowing many scenarios to be run on live data. This ensures the right decisions are made at the right time.
- Provides a detailed, accurate and realistic assessment of the risks and opportunities faced. **EROS** calculates the integrated schedule and cost impact of risks and opportunities.
- Aids in the identification of opportunities and accurate assessment of their potential benefit.
- Greatly reduces your business costs, allowing managers to set aside the correct contingency and resource for a portfolio of risk and opportunity.

Technical overview
EROS is a server-based application, written using industry standard open source software applications. **EROS** has been designed to be run from the server and therefore requires no set-up on the client machine. It requires only an internet connection and a web browser. A database extraction layer enables **EROS** to overlay any database system with little or no modification.

Licensing and maintenance costs
The product is available to buy outright or to be leased on an annual subscription basis. Both options are available exclusively from Holistic Paradigms Consulting.

Successful deployments
EROS has been deployed to medium and large-scale organisations and has provided significant and quantifiable benefits. **EROS** reports were key factors in halting the developments of Heathrow Terminals 6 through to 42 at early stages.

PART 2

'Everyone is surrounded by opportunities, but they only exist once they have been seen. They will only be seen if they are looked for.'

Edward de Bono (b. 1933), creative thinker

HOW TO FIND
NEW BUSINESS

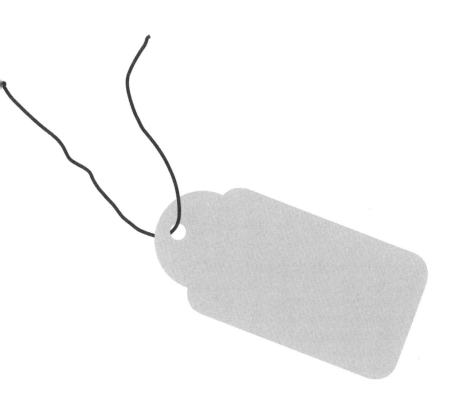

New business or existing customers?

Where should you concentrate your efforts? It is tempting to restrict your sales activity to clients you already know.

It is certainly easier talking to people you already know and it is the best way to find extra work in the short term. Working with existing clients gives you a quicker payback than finding new clients; much like sugar gives you a quicker payback of calories than some other forms of carbohydrate. For this reason, many companies make conscious decisions to focus their sales activity on existing clients and, at the time the decision is made, it is a comfortable decision to make.

However, there is danger in focusing too heavily on existing customers. If you put insufficient effort into finding new prospects then, in the medium to long term, your company will become dangerously reliant on a few key customers.

People often ask what payback should be expected from new business activity and what payback should be expected from sales activity with existing clients. Well, in the first year, new business activity will only yield about a quarter of the revenue that would be achieved with existing clients. But that is not the whole story. In the subsequent years it will usually take a lot less effort to gain extra business in the recently won account than it will in the existing account. This is because recently won accounts generally provide you with more payback for each unit of effort you put in compared to existing accounts, which are much more likely to plateau or decrease. It is simply a case of the law of diminishing returns.

So what does this all mean in practical terms? Basically that in difficult times, you should look for work among your existing clients; but in good times you should look to expand your client base.

What mixture of large and small companies should you target?

This is another common question asked in sales. The debate balances on the truism that larger accounts offer richer long-term rewards but tend to take longer to win. Smaller accounts are usually easier to win but the returns are generally lower. The answer is that in the medium to long term you will do much better targeting large companies. Size does matter.

The theory behind finding new business

The toughest part of selling is getting the initial meetings with the appropriate people. If you can do this, and so get a stream of good quality leads coming in, you will be a success. This is because, as a salesperson, you are either searching for prospects or selling to them. This means you need methods that make your searching as efficient as possible so that you maximise the amount of time you spend talking to a receptive market.

Here is an example of what 'talking to a receptive market' really means. In the early twentieth century there was a sewing machine salesperson working the American Midwest. At that time, sewing machines were a new and relatively expensive item so they were only bought by a few people. That meant that when the salesperson arrived in a new town, he knew he would be faced with the problem of having to knock on lots of doors to find the relatively few people who had the money, and the desire, to buy from him. He was spending most of his time searching for a market, not selling to a market.

Selling nowadays can seem an equally daunting task because so many companies cater for markets that are just as niche and specialised as that in our example. It is often the case that there are only a few thousand, or even a few hundred, people in the whole country who would want to buy what you offer. How do you find those people?

Well, our sewing machine salesperson came up with an interesting solution to this problem. Two weeks before he was due to canvas a town he would place an advert in that town's newspaper and advertise sewing machine repair services. People interested in these services were invited to reply to a box number with their details. When he arrived in the town, he would pick up the responses from that box number and then call on those people. In effect, he found a simple way to minimise his searching time and maximise his selling time. This is the key to success with new business. If you cannot do something like this your new business work may well prove uneconomic.

The market for what your company does might well be smaller than the market our sewing machine salesperson faced, so the next four chapters look at the most practical ways you can find prospects.

So how do you minimise your searching time and maximise your selling time?

A good starting point is to get yourself a prospect list that is at least as good as the one our sewing machine salesperson got. Thankfully, it is a lot easier to do that now than it was in the early twentieth century. In some industries there are hundreds of ready-made lists for sale.

At one end of the spectrum are lists of general contacts and at the other end are very specialised lists. You should always choose the most specialised list you can find – the list that has the very best focus on your target market. To do otherwise will always be a false economy because sales campaigns tend to make better returns the more specialised the list used.

The next chapter starts by looking at the available lists in detail. But first we should pan out for a moment and look at ...

The four main ways to find that new business

The four main channels through which you get new business are:

> mailshots

> seminars

> telephoning

> partners.

These four methods are most effective when used in mutually supporting ways. For example, a mailshot to advertise a seminar that is followed up by telephone. But before we look at how to use them together we need to know the best ways to use each of them on their own. And that is what the next four chapters are about ...

Chapter **7**

Finding new business through mailshots

- How to get good lists
- The message in your mailshot
- Knowing how many to send
- E-mailshots
- Measuring the success of mailshots
- The mailshot idea that usually fails
- Running newsletters

'You don't know a woman until you have had a letter from her.'

Ada Leverson (1865–1936), writer

The sending of mailshots is a finely tuned business working on tiny profit margins. There are basically two factors that determine whether your mailshot will be successful:

> the quality of your message (what you say)
> the quality of your list (who you say it to).

It is a common error to overrate the value of what is said and underrate the value of who it is said to.

We will look first at who you say it to. In terms of mailshots that means finding good quality, specialised lists.

How to get good lists

So where do you get good quality, specialised lists? Well, there are four main sources:

> list-broking companies
> subscriber lists from the large publishing companies (publishers of magazines and periodicals, not books)
> subscriber lists from small, specialist publications
> your company's lapsed customer list.

What should you look for in a list?

There are two factors common to all lists:

> **The level of information you want about your prospects.**
  Telephone numbers, job titles and addresses are sometimes itemised as extra costs. These extras are usually worth buying.

> **The minimum order level.** Most list brokers have one. If this is the first time you have dealt with a particular list provider it is best to buy the minimum number of names they will sell because that will give you the opportunity to examine the quality of the list before you spend (or waste) large sums of money with them.

So where should you get your lists from?

Most publishers will only allow you to rent their lists. Renting means the publisher will send the list straight to a registered specialist mailing company who will then undertake one mailing from that list for you. You will not be allowed to see the full list. Would you normally spend money on something you are not allowed to see?

A better option is to deal with those publishers who allow you to buy the list outright. This usually costs about twice as much as a one-off rental.

There are four main sources of lists:

> **List-broking companies:** These are easy to find. A quick internet search or a look through Yellow Pages will produce a number of them. For a complete list, go to any main library. Their reference section will have a book called *LADS* (*Lists and Data Sources*) which has the contact details of all the list-broking companies. If you e-mail those companies with precise details of what you are looking for you should quickly find the most specialised list available (details of *LADS*, and all the other reference sites and organisations mentioned in this book, are kept up to date on www.secrets-of-selling.com) .

> **Large publishing companies:** For many business sectors there are one or two 'industry standard' publications for the sector. For example *The Lawyer* for solicitors, *Computing* for IT, *The Grocer* for food and drink sales, and so on. These 'industry standard' publications are nearly always owned by a large publishing company, so that is the company you should first approach.

These companies can be good sources of specialised lists. They build their lists by amalgamating the names of all the subscribers to their publications and putting them into one large database. The resulting database can easily have several hundred thousand business names and those names will be available for rent or sale. Because of the large numbers involved, you will be able to take a small, specialised slice of the database.

So what are the downsides to using the large publishing houses? The limiting factor is usually that you cannot query down to job titles that are as specific as you would like. The solution to that is, of course …

> **Small, specialist publishers:** There will be small, specialist publications for your particular area of interest and they often produce excellent subscriber lists. For example, in the UK all publications and periodicals are listed in a book called *BRAD* (*British Rates and Data*) and that will be in the library's reference section too. You simply look in the index for titles that fit your target market and then contact those titles to buy or rent their subscriber list.

> **Your company's past customer list:** This is usually a small seam of leads but it can be a very rich seam. But where do you find it?

Finance will probably have details of past customers, and marketing may have details of the people who attended your company's events in the past. If neither department can help you then the records have probably been lost.

There may, on occasion, be a fifth source of lists. You can arrange to swap prospect lists with friends who work in similar, but not identical, fields. Bear in mind that you will only be able to swap names that are 'home-grown'. Lists bought from professional providers will almost certainly have been sold to you with a clause that prohibits this activity and the list will probably be 'seeded' with addresses designed to pick up on any breaches of the clause.

So much for whom you say it to. Now on to what to say to them ...

What is the message of your mailshot?

The first rule is that you should only mailshot if you have something genuinely interesting to say. It is best to be honest with yourself about this because your audience will be.

Your message could be one of many things. For this example we will look at a consultancy specialising in human resources issues that is organising a seminar in central Johannesburg for about 50 attendees. The letter promoting this seminar (Fig. 1) has a structure that is common to nearly all new business letters. That structure is composed of four parts:

> attention

> interest

> desire

> action

Most people will reply via e-mail regardless of how you send the message, but it is still best to offer several channels for reply. If you want to send out reply-paid envelopes with your mailshot you will find that sending out self-addressed envelopes with actual stamps on gets a better response than sending out reply-paid envelopes.

The people who respond positively to your mailers should be added to your database of contacts. That will allow you to gradually build up a list of your own which will, in time, become very valuable. The reason for that value is as follows. If you send out mailshots from rented lists and then measure the immediate feedback you will find that most of your mailshots are uneconomic. The value of the business you get back is less than it cost

FIGURE 1

Future Visions (Pty) Ltd
Riviona, 1630
Johannesburg
South Africa

Attention

Dear Mr Miles,

PERSONNEL UPDATE:
A summary of the latest developments in legislation and business
thought for personnel

Free morning seminars followed by lunch:
12 June – Queen Maude Centre, Johannesburg
17 June – Fountains Conference Centre, Johannesburg

The purpose of these free morning seminars is to share our knowledge of developments in the personnel sector with our clients. Non-clients are also very welcome, as we are flexible over the number of attendees, subject to a practical maximum of about fifty at each venue.

Interest

An up-to-date summary of developments in the sector will be given and there will be an opportunity to meet like-minded people from other companies over lunch. This is a pleasant and productive way to keep up to date professionally.

This seminar consists of a series of presentations and demonstrations that are designed to be useful for both personnel specialists and business executives.

Desire

The presentations will cover:
• Change management / organisational development
• Succession planning
• Assessment centre design
• Psychometric/skills profiling
• Compensation and benefits
• Executive search and selection

Note: If you do this their address must be on the side of the form they will fax back to you. Otherwise you won't know who has been accepting your invitations!

There are four easy ways to register to attend our seminars:

– Use the fax-back form on the reverse of this page.
– Register at www.mipeople.za

– E-mail me at h.bridges@mipeople.za
– Call my direct line: 27 (0) 11 779 5545

Yours sincerely,

Action

Hazel Bridges, Marketing Manager

you to win it. However, if you process all the information that comes back to you and store it in a contact management system the economics start to change. This is because some of those newly inputted names will respond positively to your next mailing and some to the mailing after that, and so on. Mailshots work on such tight margins that this type of 'asset building' can be the only thing that makes them economic.

After a while you will have built a prospect and customer list of great commercial value, almost before you realise what you have done. (Chapter 16 goes into more detail on contact management and what to do with those lists.)

How many letters should you send?

A rule of thumb is to expect the mailshotting of a list to produce approximately 50 times fewer leads than would be generated by telephoning the list. However, mailshots have the advantage of being quicker, and they need less skill and perseverance than telephoning.

To find the right number of letters to send out in a mailshot, you first need to decide how many people you want to attend your seminar. Then you just work backwards. If you mailshot to prospects who have never heard of your company the response rate will be very low. Typically, 0.25–0.35 per cent will say they want to attend an event. (That is about 1 person in 400.) Last-minute pressures of work will mean only 75–80 per cent of those people will actually show up on the day. That is about 1 in 500 of the original list. Therefore getting 50 new business attendees on the day means mailing 18,000–25,000 prospects.

However, response rates from people you already know will be a lot higher – usually between 1 and 2 per cent. About 80 per cent of these people will actually turn up on the day. So in those cases you only need to mail 2,500–5,000 to get 50 attendees.

E-mailshots

E-mail lists throw up fewer leads than postal mailshots. In practical terms this means two things:

> If you are offered a choice between buying an e-mail list or a postal list the postal list is probably better value.

> E-mailing is only economic with your own lists.

Specialist mailing companies

It is best to use a third-party mailing house for any sizeable mailing because they will be a lot more efficient at handling large quantities of mail and their hourly rates will be lower than yours. When using such companies you should seed the list so that you can audit their work.

Measuring the success of mailshots

So how do you measure the success of your mailshot? You may well use lists from several different sources for your mailshot. If so, you will want to know which source is the best value for money. The way to do that is to give a code to each list (for example 'our ref: LMK') and print that code on each letter that goes out from that particular list. The replies will enable you to determine the exact value of each list.

Determining the value of each mailshots comes down to three measures:

> the mailing date and the number mailed

> the response rate per thousand

> the cost per response.

Some general points about mailshots

> You need to decide whether to send out free gifts with your mailing. Things like calendars and diaries are evergreens here, but are rarely cost effective. Response rates improve when more expensive gifts are sent to a handpicked section of your database, but even then you will struggle to get back the money you spent on the exercise.

> Most mailshots imply the recipient can benefit financially from what your company has to offer. You can reinforce this impression by including a cheque, written out to the recipient, on which you have written an amount but not a signature. (Do remember which bit of the cheque to leave blank.) This method only works if the cheque is written out in your own handwriting on your own chequebook. It will have no impact as part of a printed mass mailing.

> When sending the mailshot it is best to omit people's job titles from the mailing. They will not notice if their title is right, but they will notice if it is wrong. And many of the job titles on mailing lists are wrong.

> Whenever possible, your mailshot should offer a stimulus for a quick reply. For example, the letter inviting delegates to the seminar mentions limited availability.

The mailshot idea that usually fails: rifleshot letters

A rifleshot letter is a letter sent to a small number of executives in the same industry – typically 10–100 (in contrast to a shotgun letter which goes out to thousands). The point of a rifleshot letter will usually be something along the lines of arranging a meeting for those executives where they can discuss an industry-wide issue at a neutral location. For example, a meeting of record company executives at a hotel to discuss informally online music sales.

This type of letter will only work if you genuinely have a very extensive network of personal contacts, and the truth is that most attempts to organise such events fail. The 'successes' take an inordinate amount of time to organise and when they do 'succeed' they usually deliver few results. So why do people organise them? The core reasons given by the organisers are usually that it seems 'easier' and 'smarter' than other methods of finding new business. The reality is that this sales method is seductive but unrewarding.

A better way to talk to a select group is to find the special interest group of a relevant association and offer to do a presentation for them. This is discussed in more detail in the next chapter.

Running newsletters

Essentially these are newsy articles written by you and sent periodically to the contacts on your database. Their success varies greatly from company to company. In the worst cases they just make more work for little return – because finding the news to put in them can be time-consuming. Done well, newsletters will keep your company in the thoughts of your contact base.

If you do run newsletters you should keep the frequency at four issues per year or lower. Any more than that and the quality of the articles, and the impact of your newsletter, will suffer.

Now that we have our list, our mailshots, and our attendees it is time to turn our attention to the seminar ...

Chapter **8**

Finding new business through seminars

- Attending other people's seminars
- Speed-networking events
- Running your own seminars
- Alternatives to full-blown seminars
- Following up after seminars

'To persuade, you should talk of interests, not reasons.'

Benjamin Franklin (1706–90), writer and inventor

Of course you can either organise your own seminar or you can attend someone else's. Let us first look at your options when attending other people's seminars.

Attending other people's seminars

Option 1: Attending seminars

A quick web search will bring up a number of companies running seminars on your subject area and there will be a number of delegates at those seminars who would make good prospects for you. The trouble is that it is not your seminar, so the only way you will get to speak with those prospects is by engaging them in conversation during the breaks. That will not bring you success.

Option 2: Sponsorship

There are some companies that specialise in organising conferences and a key source of income for these companies is the sponsorship rights to those conferences. Sponsorship typically means that your logo appears on the promotional material and you host some or all of the event. The trouble is the cost. Charges can easily range from £25,000 to £60,000 and, for that sort of money, running your own conference offers better value.

Option 3: Speed-networking events

These are events at which meetings are arranged between buyers and sellers in much the same way that meetings are arranged at speed-dating events. There are, however, two differences with business speed-networking events:

> The individual meetings last longer – typically 30–45 minutes.
> The sellers pay to attend the event but the buyers attend for free.

While the organisers of these events focus on particular sectors they all use similar techniques to match up the buyers and sellers. Most of these events aim to run with roughly equal numbers of buyers to sellers. Broadly speaking, people are matched up as shown on Figure 1.

FIGURE 1

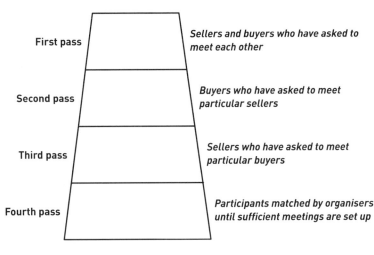

First pass — Sellers and buyers who have asked to meet each other

Second pass — Buyers who have asked to meet particular sellers

Third pass — Sellers who have asked to meet particular buyers

Fourth pass — Participants matched by organisers until sufficient meetings are set up

The real advantage of speed networking is this. To win new business economically you need to focus on the lead-generation methods that provide the most leads per pound spent. At the moment the relative costs of your lead-generation methods are probably as follows:

FIGURE 2

Common costs of different lead-generation methods

↑
Highest cost per lead
Non-targeted advertising
Event sponsorship
E-mailshots
Taking exhibition space
Mailshots
Running seminars
Telemarketing
Speed-networking events
Lowest cost per lead
↓

Once you have all your lead-generation channels running at optimum efficiency this order will change. (Particular methods work better in particular sectors.) This book will show you how to run each channel at its optimum efficiency. However, some channels will take time to reach full flow, and you would probably like an infusion of leads right now. Speed-networking events can do just that, so it is worth our looking at them in a little more detail.

How do you choose between the speed-networking events on offer?
This is made easier by the relative rarity of these events. In any given year there will only be a few that suit your company's needs.

Once you have a complete list of the relevant events, you should prioritise those that have a captive audience free from any distractions. Events held near a major city in your own country will probably suffer from people leaving early on the last afternoon. A similar problem can occur at events run at, for example, a golf course, or a hotel with unusually good leisure facilities. Events held abroad or on a ship avoid these problems.

The final differentiator between the events is this. While most organisers aim for roughly equal numbers of buyers and sellers, things happen such that some events run with a much higher percentage of buyers. Sometimes it is the organiser's policy; sometimes it is that all the sellers' places were not sold. Events like these are goldmines.

However, no good source of leads lasts forever and speed-networking, like any other lead-generation method, has built-in obsolescence. The reason obsolescence comes into play is because there are relatively few of these events. After a while you will find yourself meeting the same buyers at the same events. When that happens the law of diminishing returns kicks in.

So who should you send to these events? Nearly all the sellers attending these events do so in pairs. Of course they could attend the meetings as individuals but in practice it is not advisable. The buyers are nearly always in pairs and the pace of these events is usually too frenetic for one person to make the best of a meeting without support.

You should also send the most senior people you can. This is because the buyers will be given details about your company's representatives several weeks before the event and they will prefer to meet senior people.

The third factor in deciding who to send is one you might not readily think of. Men make up 80 to 90 per cent of the attendance at these events but analysis by the organisers shows that buyers request to meet females at roughly twice the rate they request to meet males. Therefore the female staff you send are likely to be the most successful.

Now we turn to ...

Running your own seminars

The cost of running your own seminar will probably be between £20,000 and £40,000. (A lot of the variation depends on how you view the cost of your staff's time.) However, when done as they should be done, seminars can pay you back several times over.

The purpose of seminars

The key benefit of seminars is that they allow your staff to mingle with the attendees. In practice, this means that the two most effective formats are:

> a morning seminar followed by lunch

> an afternoon seminar followed by drinks and snacks.

Either format is fine; it is the mingling that matters. The best ratio will be one member of your staff to every four attendees. (Attendees often come in pairs.) Too few of your staff means they will not get round to everyone. Too many and the attendees will feel they are being 'sold' to. The topics you choose should be about developments in your sector, not developments in your company, because the best seminars are always the ones that do not sell overtly.

Choosing the right venue

Your company will be judged by the venue you choose for the seminar, so choose somewhere upmarket. The smarter the venue, the easier it is to justify your charges. A cheap venue is usually a false economy.

When choosing a venue you should not rely on brochures and websites but visit the site in person. The best venues are often booked five to six months ahead so you will need to plan accordingly. Also, the costs of venues vary remarkably, so with a little shopping around it is relatively easy to get an upmarket venue at a mid-market price.

FIGURE 3

Choosing the right size of venue

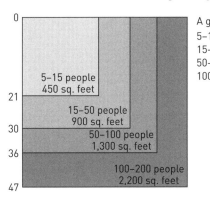

A good rule of thumb is as follows:

5–15 people	450 sq. feet	40 sq. metres
15–50 people	900 sq. feet	80 sq. metres
50–100 people	1,300 sq. feet	120 sq. metres
100–200 people	2,200 sq. feet	200 sq. metres

You will want at least two rooms. One for the presentations, and one for people to drink coffee and mingle during the breaks. You might also want storage space and a separate room for your speakers.

Choosing the right date

An easy way to maximise the audience for your seminar is to pick a date on which lots of people can attend. This is quite easy to do if you follow certain rules:

> The later in the week you hold the seminar, the more people will attend. Therefore you should choose a Thursday or Friday. However, people do not like staying late on Fridays, so afternoon events should be held on Thursdays. Morning and lunch-only events run best on Fridays.

> You need to avoid times when a higher than average number of people are on holiday. This rules out school holidays, and weeks with public holidays are also out because some people take the rest of those weeks off. December and January are bad months because people are tied up with social events in December and, for some people, January is more about organising than doing. The month in which fewest people take holidays in the northern hemisphere is November. That makes it a particularly good month for seminars.

> You need to avoid clashes with the major annual events in your profession.

When you combine all these factors with a desire to choose either a Thursday or a Friday you can see why there are so few appropriate days – about 50–60 in the average year.

When should you send out the invitations?

The ideal way is to plan to schedule a year's seminars in the preceding autumn and then advertise them by mailshot in the following way:

> In January send out a schedule of events to everyone on your list. This is effective because January is the month in which PAs spend the most time filling in their bosses' diaries.

> You then send out invitations seven weeks before each event.

When registrations come back you should acknowledge them quickly and check any dietary requirements. You should not be afraid to decline politely 'inappropriate' delegates if their attendance would reduce the quality of your audience. (The most diplomatic way to do this is to say that all the delegate places have been filled.)

In view of the long-term nature of this planning you might want to run a series of seminars that develop a particular theme. This develops a rapport with the attendees that results in repeat attendance.

FIGURE 4

Appropriate days to hold a seminar

January						
Mo	Tu	We	Th	Fr	Sa	Su
	1	2	3	4	5	6
7	8	9	10	11	12	13
14	15	16	17	18	19	20
21	22	23	24	25	26	27
28	29	30	31			

February						
Mo	Tu	We	Th	Fr	Sa	Su
				1	2	3
4	5	6	7	8	9	10
11	12	13	14	15	16	17
18	19	20	21	22	23	24
25	26	27	28	29		

March						
Mo	Tu	We	Th	Fr	Sa	Su
					1	2
3	4	5	6	7	8	9
10	11	12	13	14	15	16
17	18	19	20	21	22	23
24	25	26	27	28	29	30
31						

April						
Mo	Tu	We	Th	Fr	Sa	Su
	1	2	3	4	5	6
7	8	9	10	11	12	13
14	15	16	17	18	19	20
21	22	23	24	25	26	27
28	29	30				

May						
Mo	Tu	We	Th	Fr	Sa	Su
		1	2	3	4	
5	6	7	8	9	10	11
12	13	14	15	16	17	18
19	20	21	22	23	24	25
26	27	28	29	30	31	

June						
Mo	Tu	We	Th	Fr	Sa	Su
						1
2	3	4	5	6	7	8
9	10	11	12	13	14	15
16	17	18	19	20	21	22
23	24	25	26	27	28	29
30						

July						
Mo	Tu	We	Th	Fr	Sa	Su
1	2	3	4	5	6	
7	8	9	10	11	12	13
14	15	16	17	18	19	20
21	22	23	24	25	26	27
28	29	30	31			

August						
Mo	Tu	We	Th	Fr	Sa	Su
			1	2	3	
4	5	6	7	8	9	10
11	12	13	14	15	16	17
18	19	20	21	22	23	24
25	26	27	28	29	30	31

September						
Mo	Tu	We	Th	Fr	Sa	Su
1	2	3	4	5	6	7
8	9	10	11	12	13	14
15	16	17	18	19	20	21
22	23	24	25	26	27	28
29	30					

October						
Mo	Tu	We	Th	Fr	Sa	Su
	1	2	3	4	5	
6	7	8	9	10	11	12
13	14	15	16	17	18	19
20	21	22	23	24	25	26
27	28	29	30	31		

November						
Mo	Tu	We	Th	Fr	Sa	Su
				1	2	
3	4	5	6	7	8	9
10	11	12	13	14	15	16
17	18	19	20	21	22	23
24	25	26	27	28	29	30

December						
Mo	Tu	We	Th	Fr	Sa	Su
1	2	3	4	5	6	7
8	9	10	11	12	13	14
15	16	17	18	19	20	21
22	23	24	25	26	27	28
29	30	31				

What other written material will you need?

Mailshots consume vast quantities of paper and envelopes so you will need to order stocks of these in advance unless a mailing company is doing the work for you. Each attendee will want an information pack and you will want to ensure that all your staff have a good supply of business cards.

You will want name badges for your staff and the attendees as they aid the mingling. People dislike their name or job title being incorrect so you need to get everything right. You should have some blank name badges available to allow for these eventualities. Some companies choose to colour-code badges to distinguish between the various groups at the seminar (prospect, client etc.). Badges should be large enough to be read from 1.25 metres (4 feet) away.

Preparing your staff

Most seminars consist of senior management standing at a lectern and talking, so be thankful that your senior managers are natural and vivacious speakers. You might want to spare a thought for those speakers who could, for the sake of a few hundred pounds, get professional help with image and presentational style. It can make an enormous difference.

Hiring a well-known figure from your industry as a guest speaker will usually draw extra people to your event. When choosing between speakers, the test is whether their speaking fees are less than the cost of the mailshot you would otherwise have had to organise to get those extra attendees. (Although prestige may also be a factor for you.)

Once you have everything prepared you need to ensure that your speakers understand the running order and content of each section. If they do not, some speakers may wander into subjects that properly fit in another speaker's section. This leaves a danger that they contradict one another.

Collectively, your staff will know a lot of information about a lot of the delegates. The trick is to share that information between them prior to the event. To do this you should circulate a list of attendees to your staff and ask them to write down what they know about each one. That way they will all be in the picture come the day of the seminar.

Finally, make sure you have a reserve speaker and a reserve topic to allow for situations such as illness or technical failure.

Preparing the venue

Venues usually take care of most things for you. The only things you need to address are:

> Make arrangements to ensure your attendees do not have any problems with security or parking.

> Ensure you put up notices that make the plan of the day very clear – delegates like structure.

> Put flowers at appropriate places around the room – they will make a difference out of all proportion to their cost.

> Set up an information and message system. It need not be anything elaborate: for example, a message board in the coffee area will reduce the number of people who ring their office on their mobile during coffee breaks.

Should you get someone to organise it for you?

There are companies that organise corporate events and typically charge between 10 and 15 per cent of the total event budget. Generally, they are best used if:

> ➤ you are a very busy person, or
> ➤ the event is for several hundred people, or
> ➤ the event takes place on something that floats.

If you do not use one of these companies you can expect a seminar of the type described earlier to take about 10 days to organise.

Tips for the day

There are three things to be aware of on the day:

> ➤ You must ensure people are not kept waiting when they arrive at the event.
> ➤ You should reserve a few seats at the back of the auditorium for the inevitable late arrivals.
> ➤ Some people, both staff and attendees, are self-conscious of being seen alone during the networking times. They tend to stick to people they know rather than mingle. This is a comfortable way to network but it is certainly not the most effective. You can capitalise on this trait by actively seeking the attendees who are standing around on their own. Most of them will be feeling self-conscious and will be glad of someone to be seen talking with. That is your chance.

Alternatives to full-blown seminars

Of course, running a full-blown seminar costs a lot of money and your budget might dictate a cheaper option. In these cases you should run your seminars under the umbrella of a relevant, professional organisation. So if, for example, you want to sell to accountants you apply to be a guest speaker at their convention.

Following up after seminars

It is best to make follow-up telephone calls to all the delegates in the fortnight after the event. If you do not do this, much of the value of the event will be lost. This is because the value of sales events is reaped not so much on the day, but during the following up. Or, as Napoleon more aggressively put it, the 'best rewards' of his military efforts were not gained during his battles, but during the pursuits of broken enemies that followed those battles.

But what impedes a successful follow-up to a seminar? The most common three causes are staff being too busy in that post-event crucial fortnight, staff being telephone shy, or staff simply putting their other work first.

The main rules for following up are:

> As soon as the last attendee leaves, your staff should meet and collate all the information gathered on each attendee – things like the comments on the feedback forms, what they said to your staff, what was previously known about them and so on. This is best done while it is still fresh in everyone's mind.

> You need to assign the follow-up of particular delegates to particular staff. That makes particular staff accountable for particular delegates.

> You should follow up during the fortnight after the event, but not the day after (the day after would appear too pushy).

That is all you need to know about seminars. Another way to find new business is to use the telephone ...

Chapter **9**

How to use the telephone for selling

- The secret to selling successfully on the phone
- The four possible responses to your call
- The words you should use
- Getting past gatekeepers
- Common issues when phoning

'One of the best ways to persuade others is with your ears – by listening to them.'

Dean Rusk (1909–94), diplomat

A few home truths about selling on the phone

Most books and courses on selling describe cold calling as a situation in which the salesperson picks up a phone and goes straight through to a decision maker who talks openly about the issues affecting their business. In real life it is nothing like that.

Whether you plan to cold call or not this will be a useful chapter for you because it gives a range of tips that will make your use of the telephone much more effective. The truth is that if you want to be a star salesperson you have to be good on the phone. It is one of the most effective methods of gaining new business and it smooths the progress of the other new business methods.

Gaining appointments by telephone is a particular skill but one which can be readily learnt. This chapter details what you need to know to gain the skill. Many people are fearful of cold calling, but knowing you are going about something in the best way it can be done is a good way to reduce that fear. Here is the best way to go about it:

Know what you want to get before you pick up the phone

You should know exactly what you want to get from your call before you pick up the phone. What you are aiming for is a situation in which you are speaking with a decision maker who has a good understanding of what your company does and is happy to talk about their situation. But the other person will not just open up there and then. So how do you get to such a situation? Well, you need to start by changing your preconceptions about cold calling.

People often make the mistake of thinking that the purpose of a cold call is to sell products and services. Actually, it isn't. Its real purpose is to *sort through* the prospects and gain appointments with the appropriate ones. This means that on the phone you should only ever try to sell the appointment; never anything else. If you adopt this mindset, the time you spend on the telephone will be a lot less stressful, and a lot more productive. *It is about searching, not selling.*

The four possible responses to your call

Here is an analogy that describes this sorting process. Imagine you are a factory employee standing at the end of a production line that produces four different types of product. Your job is to pick up the product when it reaches you and put it in a pile with others of its type. When you are cold calling there are only ever four possible outcomes to each call. The outcomes are:

1 The respondent says 'Yes, I have a need for what your company offers now'.

2 The respondent says 'I may have a need for what you offer in the future'.

3 The respondent says 'No, I will never want what you offer'.

4 The respondent is rude to you.

All you need to do is identify which of these four camps a respondent falls into and then proceed accordingly.

Only about one in 100 calls will end with an option 4. Most of your calls will be option 2 or option 3. You will find yourself chancing into option 1.

So how should you react to each particular outcome?

Response 4: The respondent is rude to you

Picking up the phone again after this type of response can be difficult, but you need to put the incident to the back of your mind and call again when you have your composure back. There is nothing wrong in putting the phone down on rude prospects.

It is good to minimise the number of times you receive this type of response. The way to do that is simply to be really nice to everyone you talk to. That makes it difficult for them to be rude to you. Adopting this type of attitude will also get you a long way in the sales calls that constitute the other 99 per cent of your work.

Response 3: 'No, I will never want what you offer'

Thank them for their time and take them off your list. Do not worry if the 'nos' keep coming through. A lot of sales manuals urge you never to take 'no' for an answer but that is not what real persistence is about. The purpose of the call is sorting.

Response 2: 'I may have a need for what you offer in the future'

First, you need to ask yourself whether you think they really will have that need in the future. Frequently people just make positive-sounding statements as a polite way to get you off the phone. Is that what has just happened to you?

If you think the prospect is genuine then you need to keep in contact with them and you need to ask them about their future plans. For example, they might tell you when a contract is due to expire or when they expect to be looking for new suppliers. Say you will make a note to call them again in the future and ensure you do so. An appropriate call-back frequency is about once every three months.

Response 1: 'Yes, I have a need for what your company offers now'

If you think they will agree, ask for a meeting. However, these situations are rare because most people will want to see some information about your company before they agree to a meeting. Ringing up and asking for a meeting on the first call tends to ensure you do not get a meeting. If you wait until the second call before asking for a meeting you will be much more successful. Therefore, your best policy is usually to suggest you send an e-mail outlining what your company offers and then call back in a few days once they have had a chance to read the e-mail.

Adopting this two-call method will make it much easier for you to set up an appointment when you call back in a few days' time. It also means that the prospect, by reading your literature, will be doing some of the qualifying themselves and that makes the sorting process more efficient for you.

So what should you say?

Remember, there are two drivers behind your call: to sort through the suspects and to arrange meetings with the promising ones. Therefore your words need to reflect those two drivers and they need to be said in a way that puts the prospect at ease – a way that will make them open up about their situation.

It is important to remember that the person you are calling probably gets a lot of calls each day and they will make up their mind in the first 10 seconds whether they want to speak to you. Most of the calls they receive will be from people reading from set scripts with limited knowledge of what they are selling. Those callers will be making about 100 calls per day and they will sound bored.

Your prospect will not want to speak to many of those callers, so your call needs to sound different. The best way to do that is to make it sound as though the prospect is the recipient of a well-targeted and thoroughly researched call. Not just that, but the call is coming from someone who works in the same specialist field. Most people are quite happy to receive such calls, which are a world away from a standard cold call.

The following words will achieve that effect:

Some words for the first call

The following example uses a situation in which an IT consultancy, specialising in risk, is looking to find new customers. With purely superficial changes, the words used here would be appropriate to sell any product or service. The words assume you are calling from a list of people who have an interest in your specialism. (Advice for calling from less specialised lists is examined later in this chapter.)

> *Hello [their name], I hope I don't catch you too busy, it's just a quick call. I think you are the person I should be speaking to at [their company name]. My name is Will Cusack from a company called CMRS. The reason I'm calling is that we are an IT consultancy that specialises in risk management and I understand you are the person broadly responsible for risk at [their company name.] Is that correct?*

They will basically say they are or they are not at this stage. If they are not the person, you should ask them if they can point you in the right direction as to who to talk to. We are looking ideally for someone with money, authority and need. Or failing that, someone who is at least an influencer of decisions.

FIGURE 1

The people you are searching for

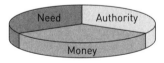

If they are the right person, then you continue:

> *I see [their name]. At this stage it's just an introductory call, nothing more. What I have is a one-page summary of our skills and services that I would like to e-mail you by way of an introduction. I don't have your e-mail address, could I ask for that?*

Most people will give you their e-mail address at this stage.

> *Thanks [their name]. I'll send that over and make a note to call you towards the end of the week to hear a little more about your situation and to see if we can match up.*

Typically, a gap three to four working days between the first and second call is an appropriate length. (We will look at what happens in that second call in just a moment.)

Examining the purpose of each line What these words are doing is working their way around two issues:

> Few people will talk about their business in depth to someone who has just called them on the phone.

> With every telephone call you should aim for the prospect to commit to something.

When we match these two issues we realise that the maximum you can expect the prospect to commit to at a first call is to read some information about your company and agree to another conversation in a few days' time. That, however, is enough for your purposes.

Let us go back to that opening line. It says:

Hello [their name], I hope I don't catch you too busy, it's just a quick call.

This is really just a polite icebreaker. It also signals a short call rather than a call from someone reading a script. It allows you to use their name. The trick to delivering this line is to keep talking into the next line because a pause at this point would ruin your chances.

Then you say:

My name is ... from a company called ...

This is there because most people open up more when they know who they are speaking to.

After that we have:

The reason I'm calling is that we are an IT consultancy that specialises in risk management and I understand you are the person broadly responsible for risk at [their company name.] Is that correct?

This makes it sound as though you only make targeted calls and the prospect is much more likely to pay attention to those calls. It has a second advantage in that it maximises the chances of them telling you who to call if they are not the correct person.

Many companies have a rule against staff giving the names of fellow workers to callers from outside the company. A way to reduce the effects of a 'no-names' policy is to use the phrase 'Can you point me in the right direction' rather than 'Can you tell me who looks after it'. People are more likely to help you if you use the first choice of words.

Few things in this world have a greater capacity to confuse than modern business jargon. Therefore in this example the words 'risk man-agement' are put in to define things more clearly. You should always avoid jargon in business, but especially when you are first trying to explain to someone exactly what it is your company does.

So what should the e-mail say?

Well, the e-mail is going to either the prospect or their PA. The company you call will either be a new prospect or a new part of a company you already do work for. Your words will change slightly, depending on the particular combination of these four factors. Here are two examples at either end of the scale.

In the first example (Fig. 2) our e-mail is going to a director's PA called Laura. The director in question is Mrs B. Careful, who is Head of Risk Management at a bank. Your company has worked for other parts of that bank, but never for her department.

FIGURE 2

Attachments: CMRS Overview   CMRS Case Study

Hi Laura,

It was a pleasure to talk this morning.

I would like to arrange a meeting between Bridget and myself. I had in mind to discuss specialised project work and the long-term supply of set numbers of staff for a specific part of the bank's work – risk management. I am conscious Bridget will first want to know a little about ourselves and our history with the bank, so here is an overview.

We have been working with the bank for the past eight years. We have always worked on risk-related projects because this is our specialist area.

Examples of past risk management work for the bank include:

- a system to report on lending risk
- a system to report on the risks and opportunities attributable to the bank's various products
- a risk management system for hedge-fund trading.

We also have an established supplier relationship with your bank. By this I mean we have a legal framework in place so that we can start work on new projects straight away. This avoids the need to get involved in lengthy contracts for each piece of work.

I attach a one-page summary of our services, plus a case study of one of our projects for the bank.

Best wishes,

J House

James House
Direct line: 64 (9) 979 7070

In contrast, an e-mail to a new prospect in a company with which you have no links would read as follows:

FIGURE 3

> Attachments: 🏛CMRS Overview
>
> Hi Paul,
>
> It was a pleasure to talk this morning. Attached is a one-page overview of ourselves. I will call you again towards the end of the week to see if there would be benefit in our meeting. I look forward to hearing more about your situation then.
>
> Best wishes,
>
> *J House*
>
> James House
> Direct line: 64 (9) 979 7070

What happens at the second call?

The aim of our first call was to ask the prospect to commit to reading the information we sent. The commitment we are aiming for at the second call is to have a conversation about their situation. If things look promising during that second call then you can arrange a meeting. The real value of a two-stage calling process is that you start the second call on a good footing.

When you make this second call people will be considerably more open to you because this time:

> they will know you
> they will know what you are calling about
> they will know you are genuine
> they will know what your company does.

This is a much-improved situation to the one you faced when you first talked to the prospect.

If you call back four days after sending the e-mail, about 75 per cent of your prospects will have read it. When someone responds with 'I've not read it yet', the best answer is usually to suggest you call back in a week's time.

This second stage will have a high qualifying-out rate because many people, having read the e-mail, will decide it is not for them. That is not a problem. After all, you are trying to sort through our prospects and the prospects that do the sorting for you are saving you time.

Others, of course, will open up about their situation and you will want to arrange meetings with some of them. In these instances it is probable that the conversation will throw up a number of hooks – topics or pieces of work you can latch on to. Something such as a requirements document, or a request for a sample.

Suggested wording for the second call The first things we need to check are that the prospect

> remembers who you are
> has read and understood the e-mail you sent
> is the correct person to speak to about this subject – i.e. in this case that they are a significant figure in risk management.

Once all that has been established, we need to open them up. The three most important things we want to find out in the 'opening-up' stage are:

> What they are doing regarding risk management at the moment.
> What they are thinking of doing/would like to do regarding risk management in the future.
> Most important of all, what their buying motives are.

The following set of words achieves all the above:

Hello [their name], I hope I don't catch you too busy. It's Will Cusack here from CMRS Group. We spoke last week about risk management and I sent you a one-page overview of ourselves – does it ring a bell?

Almost every one of your prospects will say 'yes' at this point. You might also want to add *'Is now a good time to talk?'*

You should have a note to hand of the date you sent the e-mail. This will help them find your details if they are having trouble remembering the last conversation.

Then you need them to open up. This simply means asking an open question such as:

Can you tell me a little about your situation regarding risk management, specifically what you are doing at the moment and what's on the horizon for you?

From here on you should be able to get a good, flowing conversation going. A handy measure to how well this conversation is going is to judge how much they speak by comparison with you. As with the sales meeting in Chapter 1, the ideal ratio is one in which the prospects speaks about twice as much as you do. This usually means a conversation in which questions from you lead to them opening up fully about their situation.

Arranging a meeting is easy after a conversation like that. It will seem a natural next step. Appropriate words in this case would be:

It sounds as though it would be a good idea for us to meet. Do you have a diary to hand so that we can arrange something?'

You will make more appointments if you say 'It sounds like we should meet' rather than 'Would you like to meet?' Most people will say 'yes' to the first question and 'no' to the second.

Getting past PAs

So what if a PA blocks you? Let us look first at the two most common ways people attempt to get around this problem.

> Write an unsolicited letter. Letter writing or 'sending something in' is rarely worthwhile when a PA has blocked you. Sometimes only one in several hundred letters will get a reply, and that makes it uneconomic. You can increase your chances slightly by writing the letter to the PA rather than the director. Doing so means it is more likely to be opened, read and placed on the director's desk than if you addressed it to the director.

> Phone before 8.30 a.m. or after 6.00 p.m. You can often get straight through to a prospect if the PA is not in. Some directors work long hours and are in the office very early and/or very late. Of course, this method is only useful for a short period each day.

So what is the solution then? Well, it is best to avoid the problem in the first place. Here is how. You may have noticed how easily the directors from one company seem to make appointments to see directors from other companies. They have a much better success rate than their own salespeople – but why is that? Certainly their job title helps, but that is not the key reason.

The key reason is that most directors instinctively know how to make an appointment with another director. If you copy the way they do it, you will have very little trouble with PAs. So let us look at how a director typically makes an appointment with another and see how their method differs from that of your average salesperson.

Conversations with PAs

For a start, our director knows that the other director she is calling is likely to be busy. Therefore *she asks to speak with the PA* and not with the director himself. Compare this with the salesperson who has been conditioned to talk with the decision maker at all costs.

Our director also knows that the PA has a great deal of power regarding appointments and should be treated with respect. In contrast, salespeople often try to ride roughshod over PAs – a method of operation that is certain to receive a putdown. Put yourself in the PA's position. She spends more time than most dealing with powerful egos and no amount of 'willpower' on the part of a cold caller will change her view. The situation is all the more ironic when one considers the amount of sales training that goes into 'getting past the PA'.

A call that avoids the 'willpower' method and treats the PA with respect is much more likely to motivate her to find a slot for you in her boss's diary. She will then be on your side and there is no one better suited to arranging the meeting. PAs generally know a great deal about what is happening in their departments, and that knowledge can be useful to you if they are on your side.

Arranging a time for a meeting When the time of an appointment is being discussed salespeople are usually taught to offer two alternatives. Typically they are told to say something such as 'I can make this Friday at 3.00 p.m. or next Tuesday at 4.00 p.m.' In contrast, a director making that call will know how busy the other director's diary will be and so looks for a date three to four weeks in advance. A much smoother way of doing things.

In such a situation the phrase uttered by our salesperson – offering Friday or Tuesday – merely betrays the salesperson to be more junior than the prospect they are calling. That reduces the chances of a meeting. If you suggest a date three to four weeks in advance you will give yourself more gravitas – and more chance of success.

Be ready with a slogan for their diary Your prospect is probably a busy person and there might well be a three-to-four-week delay between your telephone call and the meeting taking place. That delay could easily cause them to forget the purpose of the meeting. The PA will be aware of this and so will usually ask for a short description of the meeting to put in the diary. Therefore you should have just such a description prepared. Your description should have something memorable about it.

Treat the switchboard staff with respect too, because life is easier with them on your side. A lot of salespeople will put 10 or 20 calls, one after the other, through a company's switchboard and are then genuinely surprised when the receptionists are no longer falling over themselves to help. Alternating the companies you call eradicates this problem.

Common issues you will face when phoning

So much will depend on your list

If you call from a good quality list, upwards of 80 per cent of the people you speak to will want to hear more about what you are offering. In such situations you will be adding tremendous value to your company. However, calling from a poor quality list can be demoralising. This is one more reason why you should always go for the best quality list you can.

A common situation is to call from a list that has the names of senior people in your target company but not those of the individuals who work in your target area. When that happens you are best speaking with the PAs of those senior people and asking them for the names of the people you need.

Make sure your voice sounds enthusiastic

Having a nice tone of voice is, of course, one of your best assets as far as telephoning is concerned and cold calling is as much about presentation as it is about substance. Most appointments are made because the caller sounds knowledgeable, warm and enthusiastic. When these three factors are combined they have a compelling effect on the listener.

FIGURE 4

How you should sound on the phone

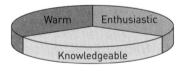

To give your call these qualities:

> ➤ You need to ensure you do not sound as though you are reading from a script. Altering your words slightly for each call will stop that happening.

> ➤ You also need to sound upbeat and interested in the prospect. Smiling will achieve that.

> ➤ You need to make it sound as though you are someone they *should* be talking to, so there needs to be a tone of assumption in what you say.

> ➤ You need to be clear. A good way to do that is to talk at 90 per cent of the speed you would talk at in a face-to-face conversation.

Make sure you are in the right frame of mind

There is little point in picking up the phone unless you are feeling upbeat and positive. Also, cold calling for sustained periods will grind you down, so you should set a time limit before you start. This should be a short limit to start with, something like 30 minutes or an hour. As your confidence and ability grows you can push that limit higher. A good upper limit is 2 hours with a 15-minute break halfway. You will need self-discipline when doing this, so tell yourself you will do the set period of time whatever happens. At regular times in that set period you should ask yourself whether you still sound knowledgeable, warm and enthusiastic. If you need to perk up, the best method is usually to perk someone else up.

Put your phone down after they have put their phone down

This is because no one likes the sound of the other telephone being put down.

Interactive voice response (IVR) systems

These systems are unlikely to be your favourite use of technology. You want to get past them as quickly as possible and, in most cases, that means pressing 0 to be put through to an operator.

But what if they are engaged?

When prospects are engaged the receptionist or PA will often ask if you would like to be put on hold. You should offer to call back instead. Time spent on hold eats into your time and means that when the other party does pick up their phone, you won't be in quite the right mindset for the conversation. (When phoning, the advantage usually lies with the person who initiates the call.)

How should you order your calls?

A lot of people find it helpful to make a batch of first calls, a batch of second calls, and so on. The reason for this is that the two types of call are best made with slightly different mindsets, and once you are in the right mindset you want to avoid repeated changes.

Phone calls are best made between 9.30 a.m. and 12.00 noon and then between 2.00 p.m. and 4.30 p.m. This is because a call will not always be well received if your prospect has just arrived in their office, or is just about to leave. Calling between 12.00 noon and 2.00 p.m. tends to be frustrating.

FIGURE 5

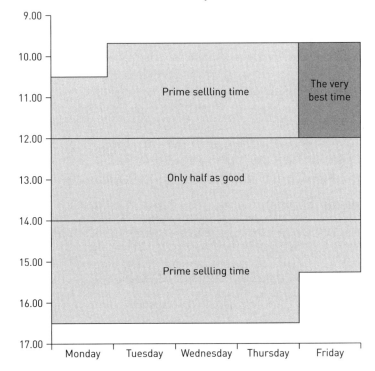

During these two hours, only about half as many people will be at their desks as at other times of the day. You are better off using this time for other tasks.

Arranging different types of calls for the morning and the afternoon can also make a difference to your success. Here is why. Most decisions in the business world are made by people in the 40–60 age range. Therefore a lot of research has been done into the psychology of selling specifically to these people. Most of it suggests they are in the most positive frame of mind to buy between 10.00 a.m. and 12.00 noon. Therefore, you should line up your most important calls and meetings for this timeslot and use the afternoon timeslot for your information gathering and cold calling.

As with all guidelines there are some exceptions:

> You might deliberately choose to ring outside these core hours to avoid a PA.

> Monday mornings tend to be unproductive times to call. Conversely, calling on a Friday morning yields above-average results (perhaps because people are in better spirits then).

> Friday until 3.00 p.m. is a good time to call to make appointments. Friday 3.00 p.m. to 4.30 p.m. is good to find out who is who in an organisation.

> Avoid calling people on their first day back from holiday, or the day before they go on holiday.

So when should you send e-mails?

People pay less attention to e-mails they receive on Friday afternoons, and those that are sitting in their inbox first thing on Monday mornings. Therefore you need to avoid sending e-mails on a Friday afternoon or first thing Monday. You should hold back from sending those e-mails until 10.00 a.m. on Monday.

You need to keep the initiative, so be wary of leaving messages

The person who makes the call usually holds the initiative but some salespeople routinely leave messages asking to be called back. Imagine it was a cold call you made and the person actually did ring you back. They would probably be annoyed to find out it was a cold call and you would have lost the sale before it even began.

When you call a prospect you may face a situation where one of the prospect's colleagues picks up the phone and says 'Can I get her to ring you back?' Your best answer in such situations is to sidestep the question. Say something like 'Thanks, but it's for me to call her, would you know when she's next available?'

What if you are calling their cell phone?

The first point to note about these phones is that they show details of missed calls, so you cannot ring them as frequently as you ring landlines without looking like a stalker.

The second point is that people answer cell phones in unusual places. Therefore you should preface your calls to cell phones with 'I'm conscious I'm calling your mobile, is now a good time to talk?' Just be aware that this is not a good question to use when making a first call to someone on a land line because it invites rejection. You should, however, still include it on second and subsequent landline calls you make to a prospect because it would be impolite not to.

What if it is really difficult to catch someone in?

Initially, you should persevere with your calls because you will get through to most people eventually. However, if you repeatedly call someone you can find that one person in the prospect's office is continually picking up the phone to you – for example, a PA or close work colleague. If this happens too often you have no option but to leave a message.

One way to reduce this is to ask the switchboard for your prospect's direct line. The only other way is to befriend the person who keeps picking up that phone. Often you can get them on your side, such that they are trying to get you to connect with the prospect too.

If you really, really cannot get through then there is no choice but a letter or e-mail. Keep this as your final option. If you have to do this, then try and get the prospect's colleague or PA on your side so that they will bring your letter or e-mail to the prospect's attention.

What if they have a no-names policy?

You have two options. One is to move on to an easier target. The other option, if the company is one you really want to break into, is to research for names. Their annual report will list the directors' names and their website may have further names. All you then need do is to speak to that person's PA and ask 'Is it Mr X who deals with this or does he delegate it to someone else?'

You need to build trust, so leave an audit trail

A person who is called out of the blue by a stranger will not immediately trust that stranger. You need to find ways to build that trust. Some of it will come from your tone of voice. Some from the words you say.

A good way to build trust with words is to give examples of past work you have done that is relevant to the prospect's current situation. Examples are always more persuasive than assertions. But the real trick is to include an audit trail. An audit trail is a set of words that give the listener sufficient clues such that they could 'trace' the story back if they chose to. This technique has a very powerful subliminal effect and is one of the keys to good storytelling. Just do it subtly, without any obvious name-dropping.

Some people believe that salespeople, as a group, lack integrity. The proper use of audit trails will help make you immune to that threat.

There is a second advantage to this method of telling stories. It means your story comes out, not in a flood, but in drips. And that will arouse your prospect's curiosity.

So you have got your appointment

The diaries of senior business people are filled with two types of appointments. First, there are 'hard' appointments – the ones they must attend. Things such as board meetings, budget meetings and so on. Second, there are 'soft' meetings. These are meetings that can be rearranged and cancelled. The appointments you make – sales appointments – will all be 'soft' meetings. It may well happen that the prospect becomes pressured for diary space and decides to cancel your appointment. If so, you should just politely keep rebooking the meeting and you are all but certain to meet in the end.

As soon as the telephone conversation with the prospect is over you should write down what was said while it is still fresh in your mind. Those notes will help you greatly in the meeting.

So how do you put all of this into practice?

The words written here are all you will ever need to know about selling on the telephone but, as the Spanish put it, talking about bullfighting is not the same as being in the bullring. You need practical experience.

A good way to consolidate your skills with the phone is to practice with calls inviting new prospects to your seminars. The main difference between this and cold calling is that instead of sending out one-page summaries of your company you are sending out invitations to a seminar. This difference makes it an ideal intermediate step.

Alternatively, you may choose to outsource cold calling to a specialist agency. When choosing an agency it is worth knowing that the most effective telemarketing teams are not necessarily those with the most experienced staff. Oddly enough the best teams are usually composed of young inexperienced callers with high morale, led by experienced seniors. The reason is that there is a fine line between experience and weariness where cold calling is involved. This particular junior/senior combination is the best solution to it. (The willingness to cold call is one of the best measures of a sales team's morale.)

Mailshots, seminars and telemarketing all give you fairly set returns for set inputs but there is another new business method where the returns are much more variable – both good and bad ...

Chapter **10**

Finding new business through partners

- The three types of partner
- How to make your partnerships effective
- How to choose the right partners for you
- How to spot the partners you should avoid
- Keeping your partnerships healthy

'You can make more friends in two months by becoming interested in other people than you can in two years by trying to get people interested in you.'

Dale Carnegie (1888–1955), writer

Three types of partner

So what exactly is a sales partner then? A sales partner is simply another company that has a hand in supplying your leads. There are three main types of sales partnership:

> **Referral partner:** For example, an architect might recommend a particular building company to his client, or a lawyer might recommend an accountant she trusts. Oddly, these types of partnerships work better when 'introduction fees' are not involved. You should only make referrals based on who you think would do a good job for the customer. It is not just that payments are unethical; it is also that by taking payments you will, sooner or later, find yourself in situations you would rather not be in. It is far better to build relationships with a range of professionals that you trust and, in the medium to long term, your sales will be better for having done so.

> **Strategic partner:** These are partnerships in which you place a consultant free of charge for six months or more with one of your major prospects in the hope of winning a large piece of work at a later date. Another example is to place your goods with a shop on a sale-or-return basis. These are high-reward options but usually entail much less risk than you would think.

> **Associate partner:** This typically means a joint venture with another company. Such partnerships lower the costs and risks of a new project but they tend to be 'fair weather' associations. If you sail into storms, your two companies can easily part.

How do you make your partnerships effective?

Partners have the potential to be your most powerful sales channel and if you run them successfully you will do extremely well. They can outstrip traditional sales channels in much the same way that companies running on franchise models tend to outstrip their more conventional rivals. However, very few companies get much revenue from partnerships and those they do set up often prove to be stairs made of sand. So what are they doing wrong?

Well, the starting point, like so much in life, is to choose a good partner. The chances are that your company's current set of partners match the 80/20 rule in that 80 per cent of the leads come from 20 per cent of the partners.

You need to adopt the approach of a dating agency in that you first need to define what you want from a partner. You should then review your current partners and ditch those that do not fit your criteria. They will take up a lot of your time for little return. You should then focus your efforts on the top 20 per cent to the exclusion of the others.

Once you have done that, you should locate the remaining companies that fit your criteria and make efforts to meet them.

But how will you know when first meeting them which companies are likely to be good partners? Well, a successful sales partnership depends on three factors. You need to judge beforehand how well you think the potential partner will do against these three factors:

> **Efficiency:** The chances are your company devotes a large amount of its resources to selling. Most companies have to do this simply because selling is the hardest part of what they do. A key measure of a good partnership is that it needs less time, effort and money to bring in a given volume of work than is needed by your standard sales methods. Good partnerships are the most efficient sales channel you have, and if a partnership does not pass the efficiency test you should drop it.

> **Mutuality:** What do you and the partner company stand to gain from the agreement? There needs to be something in it for both of you if the partnership is to work, and the gains for each side need to be reasonably equal.

> **Simplicity:** This is the third ingredient for a successful partnership. Only simple partnerships work. If the method by which you and your partner operate is even a tiny bit complex, the partnership is doomed.

So much for the theory. Let us look at one commonplace example of a successful partnership. In it, all three factors can be seen.

The IT services company

Good partnerships are commonly found in the IT industry where IT service companies often partner IT product companies. Why? Well, the product companies are usually focused just on selling the products and rarely do much of the services work that surrounds those products – the work such as installing and supporting the products. The services companies tend to do the exact opposite.

Such arrangements allow the product companies to focus on their core business and give the services companies a profitable stream of work that requires relatively little sales effort.

What sort of partnerships should you not put effort into?

Any in which the efficiency, mutuality and simplicity are not *all* present. Of course, people set up bad sales partnerships every day. An example of the most common type is as follows. Two accountancy firms are located near to each other. One specialises in business tax, one in personal tax. They recommend each other's services from time to time but there is no strong bond there. The only time this type of partnership works to any degree is when there is a pre-existing relationship, such as a family link, or both parties knowing each other at school.

You should avoid spending time on partnerships like this because they are rarely more than comforting illusions.

Make sure you look after the good partners

You need to give something to the relationship so that it keeps giving to you. What you give depends on the particular partner. For example, it might be that a particular industry expert is recommending your company from time to time. Such people are in the public eye more than most and so they value their reputations more than most. Therefore the best way to pay back such a person might be to do something that enhances their reputation. Whatever it is they value, the important point is to look after them.

Now that you know how to ensure a steady source of leads comes through, the toughest part of your job is over, and your success is all but assured. But selling is not just about doing well at meetings, writing good proposals and finding new business. To be a complete salesperson you need to know how to act in the other situations that arise ...

PART 3

'Not on one strand are all life's jewels strung.'

William Morris (1834–96), writer, artist and political activist

BECOMING A
COMPLETE
SALESPERSON

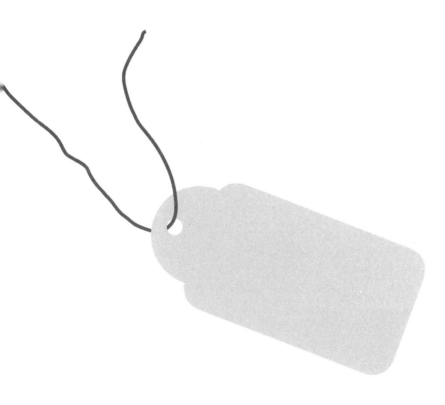

Chapter **11**

How to brand and advertise your company effectively

- How to create a brand
- Colours and branding
- Advertising
- How to choose a tagline
- How to place your adverts
- Dealing with advertising agencies

'Sanely applied advertising could remake the world.'

Stuart Chase (1888–1985), economist

Good branding is worth a fortune. Just think of the brand value of Coca Cola, Nike, Levi's or a whole host of consumer products. Brand is the single most valuable thing these companies possess and it is literally worth billions to them. Service industries have, in general, been a lot less smart about the way they promote their brands. A few, such as McKinsey's, have got some of the way there, but most fall far short of what can be achieved.

How do you create a good brand?

There are five cardinal rules to branding. To save you having to work them out from scratch, here they are:

> ➤ The most common mistake is to develop your brand with a view to creating a particular mood. People see through this technique and conclude the brand is more about style than substance. A better approach is to create a brand that has a unique identity. Do that and everything will fall into place behind that identity.

> ➤ The more you can associate your company's name with a specialist area, the stronger your brand will be. For this reason, names like Universal, Standard or General will not be the best ones available to you.

> ➤ Short names work better than long ones.

> ➤ PR and the media are the most cost-effective ways to launch new brands. Advertising works best for more mature brands.

> ➤ Your name should suit all countries. For example, the US chicken brand of 'Frank Purdue' once had the slogan 'It takes a tough man to make a tender chicken'. The nuances of translation meant this slogan caused widespread consternation in the Mexican market. (Further sales blunders are listed on the website that accompanies this book.)

Which colour best suits your brand?

The colours in your brand and logo significantly affect the image of your company. So which colours should you choose? Well, before we answer that, we first need to understand how colour affects psychology.

Colour is composed of light travelling at different wavelengths – each wavelength creating a slightly different colour. For example, red is created by long wavelengths, blue by short ones. This means that red light strikes ahead of the retina and the adjustment we make for this means that red appears to move towards us. Blue light strikes towards the back of the retina and so appears to move away from us. Green lies in the middle of the spectrum and needs no adjustment. These adjustments to your retina are picked up by nerves that send messages to your brain. The way your brain processes these messages causes us to react to different colours with different emotions.

In a moment we will look at tips for choosing colours for your business. Before we do, we should summarise the way in which each colour affects emotions.

> **Red** is the most stimulating colour. It conveys energy and excitement and has a strong visual impact. It is the most commonly used colour in business. (One reason you might want to avoid it.)

> **Blue** is primarily associated with dependability, stability and tradition, but has secondary associations with reason, logic and deep thought. (For example, Big Blue, the nickname for IBM.) The downsides of blue are that it can make your company appear cold and reserved. It is the second most commonly used colour in business.

> **Orange** is the most schizophrenic colour, denoting both caution and warmth. In business it proved spectacularly successful for the mobile phone company and poor for just about everyone else who tried it. It is also the most discordant colour, which is why few people look good in orange clothes and why it does not complement any other colours.

> **Yellow** is the brightest colour and the one we associate most closely with emotion. Depending on its intensity yellow implies mature self-confidence or jaunty arrogance. It also has associations with creativity and, in its gold shade, with success. Creativity, success and emotional maturity are excellent qualities for your company to exude.

> **Black** is associated with luxury when applied to products, but it is wholly unsuitable for service industries that do not involve killing people.

> **Grey**. No one in their right mind would use grey.

> **White** is, of course, associated with innocence and purity. Commendable qualities in themselves but are they appropriate for promoting your business?

> **Purple** has strong associations with religion and for that reason is best avoided as a corporate colour.

> **Green** is of course associated with the environment and health. Research strongly indicates it is the best colour to choose for backgrounds because people are most drawn to an item or a logo when it is placed on a green background.

Some general rules for choosing colours It may be that your company is a pioneer in a particular market. If so, you should choose a colour for your company that best symbolises that market. For example, a supplier of leading edge electrical goods should choose electric blue. A family law firm should choose green.

If you only have one major competitor you should generally choose the colour that contrasts most strongly with that competitor. For example, Coca Cola chose red so Pepsi chose blue.

Advertising

Product companies have achieved much more with their branding than service companies have and the same is true with advertising. There is a conspicuous lack of famous taglines associated with service companies to date.

How do you come up with a good tagline for a services company?

An ideal tagline for a company selling services would have four key elements:

> First, it needs to imply value. John Lewis's 'Never knowingly undersold' is a good example of this.

> Second, the line would need to imply your company's staff are the experts in their particular field. 'Let's make things better' by Phillips does just that.

> Third, trust needs to feature prominently. 'Never knowingly undersold' is the best example here too.

> Finally, the tagline should take a leaf from McKinsey's book. They have a rule that they will only ever work for a client if McKinsey's can add more value by doing that work than they take away in fees. Converted into a tagline, this rule would be compelling.

If you ever come up with a tagline that includes all four of these elements you will have done an outstanding day's work for your company.

Some less important rules about all taglines are that they should

> be memorable – not bland or general
> include benefits and be phrased in the positive
> include your company name
> say what you or your product does
> differentiate you from the competition
> not be usable by the competition
> not sound too corporate, pompous or smarmy.

Where should you place your adverts?

The overriding issue with advertising is to find a form of advertising that is economic – a form that produces more leads than the cost of the advert. To help you achieve that you need to understand a little about how people read publications. A lot of research has been done into this, and the main conclusions are as follows:

> The closer your adverts and articles are to the beginning of the publication, the more they will be read. This is because people tend to read the beginning of a publication more fully than they read the later parts. If you are placing an advert and the publisher's contract mentions 'TOP' (terms of placement) it means they keep the right to place the advert wherever they choose in the publication. In practice, most will negotiate if you ask.

> Adverts on the right-hand side of the page are read by more people than those on the left. The very best position is the bottom right-hand corner.

> Adverts do better when they face a page that has editorial on it, rather than another page of advertising. This is because people tend to skip pages they think have 'too much' advertising.

> In a column of adverts, those at the top are read more than those at the bottom.

> Typically only 25 per cent of readers read past the headline of an advertisement, so you should concentrate your efforts on that headline.

> Research indicates that putting a line space between paragraphs increases readership by about 10 per cent (because it makes the text look less daunting).

> Colour advertisements are generally read by about twice the number of people who read black-and-white advertisements.

However, most publications do not double their charges for colour, so it usually makes sense to go for colour.

> Photographs and artwork attract about twice as much attention as written text, so they are worth including.

> Photographs tend to be about 25–30 per cent more effective than artwork (because people believe the camera is less likely to lie).

> The size of the advert is also important. One might assume that the larger the advert the greater the response, but the actual responses follow the pattern below (first described by the statistician Philip Sainsbury).

FIGURE 1

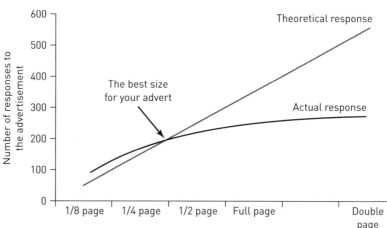

The best size for your advert

The trick is to size your advert so that it hits the point highlighted on this graph. Broadly speaking, that point will be about a third of a page for a tabloid-sized publication. It will be slightly more for a broadsheet, and slightly less for magazine size.

What do advertising agencies do?

Advertising agencies do some, or all, of the following:

> They research and advise on the markets and media channels most suitable to you.

> They create your advertisements.

> They place your advertisements for you, often at lower rates than you could get.

The charges of advertising agencies tend to be opaque. As well as charging you, they may also take a payment from the publications in which they place adverts. When you are agreeing charges with an advertising agency the most practical route is usually to agree a figure that is not to be exceeded.

Having your branding and advertising sorted will improve the effectiveness with which you address large groups of people. But how do you best address large groups of people in person? Well, there are ways to do it well ...

Chapter **12**

Presentations, away-days and exhibitions

- The best ways to present
- Things to remember when you are preparing to present
- Things to remember when you are presenting
- How the size of the audience affects your presentation
- Client away-days
- Manning an exhibition stand
- Following it all up

'Never overestimate your audience's knowledge; never underestimate their intelligence.'

C.P. Scott (1846–1932), newspaper editor

This chapter gives you lots of tips for effective presentations, but, first, one caveat needs to be given. For many people, the key trick to presenting well is about controlling their fear of public speaking – a common phobia. Just as with cold calling, knowing you are going about something in the best way it can be done is a good way to reduce that fear. Here is the best way to go about it.

The best ways to present

The trick to making a presentation is to make it sound like it is about them, not you. There are some practical steps you can take to achieve this. Here they are:

Things to remember when you are preparing to present

> Preparation swallows large amounts of time. Typically you should plan your presentation using a ratio of 15:1, i.e. you should expect to spend 15 minutes preparing for each minute of actual presentation.

> Graphs and charts make for better presentations than words, so include all you can. But they must not be too dense.

> Avoid bold lettering in presentations – it looks like you are shouting at your audience.

> Choose the right colours. Dark shades of blue, black and red are the easiest colours to see on a computer screen. Yellows and browns are problematic and it is likely that some of your audience will have sight problems. Also, reading speeds will be slowed if you use any set of colours other than black print on white background. (Research suggests that bad colour combinations reduce reading speeds by about 40 per cent.)

> Prepare a start that will grab your audience's attention, but save your best till last. They will remember your presentation by its ending, not its beginning.

> It's always worth practising beforehand, especially if technical demonstrations are involved.

> The ratio to remember for screen size is 7:1. This means that if your audience is sitting 7 metres (23 feet) from the screen; the screen should be 1 metre (40 inches) wide to be seen easily. If people are having trouble seeing your presentation they will quickly lose interest. On a similar note, you should prefer landscape format. It fits the eye better than portrait.

- On the day you should get to the presentation room ahead of time. Once there you should set the seating plan to your preferred layout and ensure you understand how the air conditioning works.

Things to remember when you are presenting

- You should start with a question but be careful how you phrase it. The ex-British Prime Minister Tony Blair once started a presentation to his party by asking them what they would like to hear him say. 'I resign' was the shout from the back of the room.

- As soon as you can you should give your audience a roadmap of what it is you will talk about. Then, as you go through your presentation, you should periodically tell them where you are on that roadmap.

- When presenting, you normally have to fit into a neat time slot and overrunning that time will irritate the audience. A good rule of thumb for measuring presentation time is to allow two minutes to talk through a standard slide, and four minutes for a slide that has a lot of technical content.

- You need to ensure there is no aspect of your appearance or delivery that could invite ridicule, but you also need your personality to show.

- Only use humour if you are naturally humorous. Think how people cringe at bad comedians on stage. The main target for humour should be yourself. Humour targeting at the audience or the competition is usually a quick route to self-destruction – unless you are very, very funny. Jokes are better when shared rather than made.

- When a slide appears you should read what it says (very few presenters actually do). If you do not, your audience will read it – and what you say while they are reading will be lost.

- Remember that you do not have to fill every moment with sound. Pauses are very effective when presenting and a well-timed silence will make a powerful noise. The pause will usually sound longer to you than the audience.

- As with the telephone, you should talk at 90 per cent of the speed you would talk at in a face-to-face conversation.

- When you want to highlight something, point at the board, not the computer screen (a lot of presenters point at the screen).

- Do not use a long pointer or a lightstick when presenting. They attract attention to themselves, and away from what you are saying.

For the same reason you should avoid using the most eye-catching features of PowerPoint. All they do is highlight the features of PowerPoint.

> It is best to provide handouts of the slides before you start. People will write your comments down against the appropriate slides as you speak, which means more information will be conveyed from you to them. Providing handouts also helps those members of your audience who have sight problems.

> When you finish you should not just stop speaking and get down from the podium. You should sum up the main points and make it clear that you have finished. Try and tie the end to the beginning.

How does the size of the audience affect your presentation?

If you are presenting to one or two people you will be more persuasive using printed slides than you will be with a computer. This is because people are more likely to believe what they see on paper than what they see on a computer screen. They find it more personal too.

It is difficult to achieve the same degree of intimacy when presenting to large groups. The next best thing you can do is maintain eye contact with the individuals making up your audience. Try to make eye contact with every member of your audience at least once during your presentation.

Client away-days

An away-day is an event to which you invite several clients or prospects from the same company. The idea is that they spend the day with you away from their office. Usually, this means a nearby hotel. These events are very powerful sales tools because they give you valuable time with your prospects, free from any distractions. It is much the same effect as that achieved by the speed-networking events that are held away from distractions. They allow you to gain the trust of the client, and a deeper understanding of their buying motives.

Do not be tempted to stage the event at their offices, even if they make that offer. Your prospect will meet a steady flow of your competitors in their own offices and, over time, the faces of those competitors will start to fade into the backdrop of the office wall. However, by contrast, the day you spend at the hotel will stay imprinted on their mind for much longer. However, be aware that away-days are an expensive tactic, best reserved for situations where a lot is at stake.

Managing an exhibition stand

So you are going to be on an exhibition stand. There are six things to remember when on an exhibition stand. Here they are:

➤ **You are there for the conversation:** The actual reason for having the stand is that it gives you the opportunity to converse with potential customers. A lot of exhibitors rather lose track of this and see it instead as an opportunity to hand out promotional items indiscriminately.

➤ **Use coffee to attract people to your stand:** One of the best ways to get into conversation with potential prospects is to offer free coffee at your stand. It takes a few minutes to drink and the smell will attract more people to your stand in the first place. You should always use china cups instead of paper ones because people are more likely to walk off with the paper ones and visit other stands. The cost of the coffee, and a few lost china cups, is far less than the cost of the gimmicks that are typically given away at exhibitions.

➤ **Talk about the attendee, not yourself:** Chapter 1 looked at the importance of talking *with* rather than *at* someone – the need to talk about the prospect's situation rather than your company's features. Nowhere is this advice more enthusiastically ignored than at exhibitions. There is something about being on a stand that makes salespeople think they should gush forth about their company without once asking the prospect what their buying motives might be. It is the same syndrome that leads to that excess handing out of promotional items. The truth is that prospects need to be listened to wherever they are.

➤ **Watch your posture:** People on trade stands, particularly men, tend to stand with their hands clasped behind their back and their feet slightly apart. This makes them look like security guards at just the time when they should be looking welcoming. If you find yourself adopting this stance, make a conscious decision to change to something more relaxed and welcoming.

➤ **Collect the contact details of your customers:** Nowadays, most exhibition organisers offer a system that allows you to scan the barcodes on the badges of people visiting your stand. However, it

131

could be days or weeks before you actually get this information and some of the visitors to your stand will dislike being scanned anyway. Therefore always swap business cards. It also means your visitors take away something too.

> **Follow it all up:** Just as with seminars, the value of exhibitions is reaped not during the day but during the follow-up. The difference is that exhibitions need to be followed up as soon as you get back to the office. This is because the other exhibitors will be calling those same prospects, so you need to contact them before they are overwhelmed by phone calls.

If you follow all these tips, exhibitions will become a fruitful source of leads.

Presentations, away-days and exhibitions allow you to speak to large numbers of prospects, sometimes hundreds at a time. As you progress in your career there may be times when you deal with the media and when that happens you will, effectively, be speaking to tens of thousands of prospects.

Most salespeople find their first contact with the media comes in one of two ways. It is either through an inventive attempt to stretch a marketing budget or an approach by the media to comment on something. In both cases there are things you can do to help yourself make the most of the opportunity ...

Chapter **13**

Getting the most from the media

- Getting articles into the press
- Finding journalists and publications that specialise in your area
- Press releases
- Other ways of contacting the press
- Doing media interviews
- Dealing with adverse publicity
- PR agencies
- Professional associations

'Newspapers are unable, seemingly, to discriminate between a bicycle accident and the collapse of civilisation.'

George Bernard Shaw (1856–1950), playwright

Imagine how a stream of positive comments from the media would benefit your company. It is fairly easy to achieve. The starting point when dealing with the media is to understand that people trust editorial content more than they trust adverts. And often you can get positive editorial content without paying for it.

Getting articles into the press

There are two main ways in which you can get articles about your company published in the media: you can send finished articles to editors of specialist publications or you can provide journalists with the information they need to write the articles themselves.

Method 1: Sending finished articles to specialist publications

So what exactly should you send? Well, the two things that most impress editors are innovative ideas and solid research. If your article has both, you are likely to be published. Most editors look for something about 1,500 words long (1,500 words is about two sides of A4 paper).

When submitting articles you should be wary of deals about 'advertorial'. These are deals whereby your articles are printed in exchange for you buying advertising space in the publication. The way to avoid this is to speak with editorial staff rather than advertising salespeople.

Method 2: Providing the journalists with the information they need to write the articles

This basically means you provide skeleton articles that can be adapted or edited by journalists. This process is often called syndication and its greatest advantage is that it allows your audience to read about you in more than one place. The 'same' story can appear in a number of different publications without loosing credibility, because each journalist has put their own feel to the text.

When you have your syndicated article prepared you should send it to all the relevant media. The covering letter for such articles should always be a soft sell, not a hard one. Broadly speaking, it should say that you understand they are a publication specialising in your area and they might want to write about this subject. In a moment we will look at examples of these letters. Like sown corn, some will land on fertile ground while others will lie dormant for a while before being taken up.

Your one-page overview and your case studies will provide the basic material for such an article. However, the most important extra ingredient is an 'angle' for the story, i.e. you need to present the journalist with something innovative and interesting about your company.

The 'syndication' method has three main advantages over the 'sending finished articles' method:

> It allows the journalist to claim the article as their own. (If the journalist is getting full credit for an article they will put more into it)

> It puts a professional edge on the article. Most journalists write well and they know how to make a story interesting.

> You are less likely to get entangled in 'advertorial'.

Things to remember about articles

There are five other things to mention on the subject of writing articles for placement:

> You tend to be more successful when you know which form of media you are writing for before you actually start writing. Just think how a story seems so different in a tabloid to one in a broadsheet, or how it can be changed by the political slant of a newspaper.

> Your articles will do better if they are sent with accompanying photographs and diagrams. The explanatory notes for these accompaniments need to be particularly clear because that is what the journalists will focus on.

> Be aware that photos tend to get lost when sent to publishers, so you should make copies beforehand.

> When your articles appear in print, ring up the publisher and ask them to post you some copies. (These are usually called voucher copies and are always useful.)

> The BBC has its own syndication service. It records interviews in London that are distributed around the BBC local radio network. Regional media, whether print, radio or TV, relies quite heavily on syndicated material.

Finding journalists and publications

There are probably only a few journalists and publications that specialise in your area so you only need focus on those few. Once you have their details you can approach them in several ways: for example by inviting them to your seminars or by sending details about your company, mentioning your willingness to provide an interview, article or quote when they need one.

Here are two example cover letters for syndicated stories:

FIGURE 1

Dear

I see you have written several times on the subject of security. Therefore I would like to bring our company's services to your attention in case you would like to write about them.

Inside Security specialise in the financial sector. We have developed a unique approach to the provision of security services that leaves our clients with a radically different understanding of the word 'security'.

Would you like to write about this innovative new service? If so, I would be pleased to arrange an interview. I will call you in the near future to hear more about your situation and look forward to talking with you then.

Yours sincerely,

FIGURE 2

Dear

I understand you edit a publication specialising in accounting matters.

We are a provider of accounting services and have recently developed some innovative services that may be of interest to your readers.

Would you like to write about these services? If so I would be pleased to meet with you. I will call you in the near future to hear more about your situation and look forward to talking with you then.

Yours sincerely,

So where do you find these journalists and publications that focus on your specialist area? You can, of course, use *BRAD*, the directory mentioned in Chapter 7 (on mailshots). Or a local equivalent. You can also use a computer system called InfoTrac, which is free and in most libraries. This system records articles published in UK national papers, along with the name of the journalist who wrote the article. It works like an internet search engine. You simply put in a key word or phrase such as 'probate law' or 'selling pharmaceuticals' and you will get a list of most of the journalists who have written articles on those subjects in the national press.

Besides these sources, there are specialist media directories that list all the details you need – details such as the names and job titles of particular journalists working for particular publications, and so on. The best known are:

> *Benn's Media Directory*
> *Editors Media Directory*
> *PR Planner*
> *PIMS Media Directory.*

There are two main drawbacks to these directories. First, they are not in all libraries and are expensive to buy yourself. Second, the information they contain deteriorates as people move jobs, so you need a reasonably up-to-date copy.

There are also publications that list forthcoming features on TV and radio. These are useful in that you will get advance notice of programmes focusing on your area and the editors of those programmes will no doubt be pleased to hear from you. The best of these publications is *Programme News*.

Press releases

Press releases are usually less effective than syndicated features but they are easier to mass-produce. Because Chapter 6 covered tips for writing sales documents this next section will only list tips that are particularly relevant to press releases.

Good press releases have the following characteristics:

> The information they contain is genuinely new. A tremendous amount of 'news' is simply information recycled by journalists from other news sources. There is no point writing a press release based on recycled news because journalists will not be interested.

> The story has an interesting angle.

> The release gets straight into the story. You do not need to set the scene.

> The release makes sense when you skim-read it first time through.

> The story is in the first paragraph. (Because if it is not there, the journalist will not read on looking for it.)

> The headline is interesting.

> The release has an economy of words – getting the maximum meaning from the fewest words.

> The release just has facts that are written in a news-like tone.

> The document is on one or two pages of A4, with your contact details clearly visible, the phrase 'news release' printed at the top, and a date.

> The release is no more technical than it has to be. Technical terms alienate most readers.

Good releases do not include:

> A quote from a senior director. These quotes always sound pompous and can give the impression that they were written by a PR department over-anxious to flatter that particular director.

> Unsupported claims like 'market-leading service' or 'ground-breaking'. Journalists dislike such phrases because they see it as their job to put angles on things and they do not like being 'spun' to. Most PR departments fall into this trap, but journalists have a nose for spin.

> Similarly, journalists would rather do humour, style and emphasis themselves, so do not underline or embolden anything.

So when should you send out your press releases?

> Press releases issued in the morning do better than those issued in the afternoon.

> Generally, press releases do best when released on a Sunday or Monday because there is less competing news on those days. (Newspapers work a day behind, so news released on a Sunday will feature in Monday's paper. For that reason Monday's papers are nearly always the thinnest of the week, because little news happens on a Sunday.)

> Press releases issued on Fridays are the least effective. This is because the news will be covered in Saturday's papers which have

a smaller and less business-oriented readership than the weekday papers.

> Wednesdays and Thursdays are mediocre days for press releases. A lot happens in Parliament and the law courts on those days, so there is more news to compete with.

> If you are looking to contact a weekly or monthly publication, the best day to approach them is the day after an issue has gone to press. That is the time when journalists are most focused on finding new stories.

> News released on public holidays often gains good coverage because of the lack of competition. The period between Christmas and New Year is also good for the same reason.

> Your company's work is probably linked to a particular date in the calendar. For example, tax specialists are linked to the beginning of the tax year. If such a connection exists with your firm, you should use it, because the media like topical stories.

Occasionally, press releases are issued with an embargo that prevents them being published before a certain date. Embargoes are usually respected, but you need to be a bit worldly wise when you use them. They are best used if the story is a complex one for which the journalist needs to do extra research before they publish their article.

Finally, you should remember that the more frequently you send out press releases, the less effective they become.

Press release agencies

There are agencies that act as central clearing houses for press releases. The best known of these is the Press Association, a mutual association owned primarily by the major newspaper companies. (You have probably seen the initials PA at the end of some newspaper stories. Those initials mean the Press Association was the original source of the story.) It is usually a good idea to include these agencies when you send your material out.

Other ways of contacting the press

Of course, you do not need to rely on press releases. The other main ways in which you can get into the press are:

> press conferences and media briefings

> photo opportunities

> training days for journalists.

The question you need to ask yourself before organising any of these is whether it is the best communication method for the job. Here are a few pointers to help you make that decision.

Press conferences and media briefings

You have to have a very worthwhile story to justify a press conference, and the story needs a timeliness to it. Therefore press conferences are rare in business; more common are media briefings. These are more sedate events to which you invite just a few chosen journalists.

Photo opportunities

If you have a story that would make a good photo it is best to invite the media to you, rather than send them a photo you have taken. The media always prefer to take their own photos, not least because they do not want to use a photo that appears in a competitor's title. The best photo opportunities are usually with local charities. However, things such as work experience for local students or paying for local hospital equipment show your company in an equally good light and can easily make it to the front page of local newspapers.

Training days for journalists

These are free days for journalists who specialise in your area. Typically they are updates on developments in your profession; things such as legislative changes, new technology and so on. There will only be a few journalists specialising in your sector, so it is a good idea to be friends with as many of them as possible. That way some of them will think of you when they are writing and will turn to you for a quote or interview.

Be aware that journalists are naturally curious people and there might be a few 'scoops' about your company you would rather they didn't publish. For that reason you should never let a journalist nose around your offices unless you, and your staff, are ready for that tour.

Whatever you do with the press, follow it up

In Chapter 7 (on mailshots) we noted that only 75–80 per cent of attendees who say they will attend an event actually do so. The figures are always a bit lower with journalists – typically 70 per cent turn up.

As with seminars and exhibitions the best prizes are to be won in the following up you do after the event.

Media interviews

Here is a guide, from beginning to end, as to what you should and should not do when talking with the media.

When you are first invited to a media interview you should try and find out:

> who else will be appearing

> who is the target audience

> what is the likely length of the interview

> whether it is live or recorded

> exactly which media the programme will appear on.

Find out a little about the interviewer

On a few occasions, the interviewer is following a storyline that will not reflect well on you and you need to be aware of that possibility. When these occasions happen, the interviewer's motives are rarely the result of malice, and more usually misunderstanding. The best way to defuse these problems is to talk with the interviewer beforehand and ask:

> what they think the story is about

> which angle they intend to pursue

> which areas they want to discuss

> what their first question will be.

If you have asked these questions and still have concerns about the interviewer you might want to check transcripts of their past interviews. That will soon show you what type of interviewer they really are.

Preparing for the interview: what you say

The biggest problem you face with media interviews is lack of time. You cannot lengthen the timeslot, so you should try and make every second of it work in your favour.

The first thing to do is anticipate the questions. Then you need to pre-pare your answers. When preparing those answers you should decide on the top three points you want to get across. The trick is to merge those points into your prepared answers.

Once you have the main thrust of your answers prepared, you need to think about how you will convey them. You need to do that as simply as possible. Ideally each point should be condensed into a sentence or soundbite. Indeed many writers see the encapsulation of an idea into a short and memorable phrase as the acme of good English.

If you are taking part in a radio interview it is fine to take in prepared notes with you. Just remember that notes for radio interviews should only ever be notes, never lines of text. The listeners can tell if you are reading from a script and that ruins your credibility. Second, any notes need to be written on card rather than paper. The sound of paper rustling while you answer a question is another surefire way to destroy your credibility.

Listeners can also tell if you are nervous or flustered. To reduce this danger make sure you arrive early at the venue and take a few deep breaths before the interview starts.

It is good to tell stories during media interviews, but make sure they are short and personalised.

So much for what you say, now we need to look at how you say it ...

Preparing for the interview: understanding interviewers

Interviewers most commonly trip people up with the *way* they ask their questions, not with *what* they ask. The most common technique to do this is to impale the subject with the second question. This is done by asking an easy first question to which the interviewee gives a fulsome answer that exposes their position. The second question then pushes the interviewee towards contradicting their answer to the first question, thereby appearing hypocritical, or testifying against themselves.

The technique relies upon the fact that, unknown to the interviewee, the questioner already knows the true answer to the second question and has hard evidence to support it. (The technique is used a lot by barristers. Indeed barristers have a saying that you should never ask a question in court to which you do not already know the answer.)

A second common trip-up is to ask a question that obviously needs a 'yes' or 'no' answer. The question is asked in such a way that its meaning is not obvious until the last word is said and that gives you very little time to react. The pause while you think about your answer can easily make you appear flustered or untrustworthy.

How you answer the question Politicians tend to fall into a particular trap during media interviews and it is one you should avoid. They prepare their soundbites before the interview, but a lot of them do not anticipate *how* the questions will be asked. Instead, every 'answer' they give is no more than an opportunity to get another soundbite in, regardless of what the questioner actually asked. To the listener this comes across as arrogant and sleazy. It is far better to give a straight answer to any reasonably straight question. People will respect you for it. They instinctively know that those who moralise (politicians) and those who have morals (normal people) behave very differently in their personal lives. You have to position yourself firmly with the normal people.

What to say and do during the actual interview

As with the preparation, interviews boil down to two things: what you say and how you say it. What you say is about information. How you say it is about emotion.

What you say

> Your key aim is to get your points across clearly in the time available.

> If the interviewer says anything incorrect, you should correct it immediately. Otherwise, you will be open to the charge of 'Why did you not say so at the time?'

> Finally, you need to avoid any sort of industry jargon. (This is very easy to slip into if you are nervous or defensive.)

How you say it When people first appear in a media interview they usually come across as more wooden than they are in real life. (People do much the same thing in court.) This is unfortunate because what you should be doing is projecting your personality and giving your answers with humanity, enthusiasm and measured emotion. Within reason, the more you alter the pitch and tone of your voice, the more interesting your speech is. This paints a picture in the mind of the listener and will help win the 'human' side of the argument.

As with so much in selling, media interviews are won more by emotion than by logic. That means people will side with the nice person if they possibly can. Also people will notice you if you speak with integrity, conviction and personality. People's choices when buying things are a lot about who they perceive has the most integrity and conviction

Remember that the audience is predisposed to like you. There are really only three things that can turn the audience against you. They are:

> arrogance

> smarminess

> aggression.

If you avoid these three things the interview is almost certain to benefit you.

You should also know that the biggest media disasters invariably happen when you are talking to someone who you think is on your side.

There is a phrase, often used in parliaments, that sums up this trap: 'The opposition sit opposite you. Your enemies sit behind you.' In this, as in so much of life, our greatest agonies are usually caused by ourselves, or by those we most trust.

What to wear for TV interviews

A key aspect of TV interviews is to look the part. For example, lawyers look best when interviewed either outside a court, or sitting behind a desk with a bookcase behind them and dressed in a dark blue suit. All they need do then is project an avuncular style to appear as the competent and friendly side of the law. That will be a memorable and positive image.

What not to wear for TV interviews Some patterns simply do not look good on television. The worst are small checks and narrow stripes, which can be very painful on the eyes. You should avoid some colours too. For example, white clothes can be very reflective under harsh TV lighting (and few people look good in white anyway). Expanses of black create different lighting problems, so you should avoid those too.

Accessories If possible you should avoid wearing glasses on TV because the viewers will want to see your eyes. It is particularly important to avoid tinted glasses as they can look dishonest. If you must wear glasses make sure they are clean, as smudges on the lenses show up under bright studio lights. Also jewellery can cause bright flashes under studio lights, so it needs to be discreet.

What not to do on TV

> Do not look at the camera directly. It looks awful. Keep your gaze strictly on the interviewer.

> Do not point your finger on TV because it looks even more aggressive than it does in real life.

> Avoid fidgeting.

> Avoid any unusual mannerisms. TV highlights them in the way that schoolchildren highlight the mannerisms of their teachers. There should be no aspect of your appearance or delivery that could invite ridicule.

After the interview

Do not relax your guard until the journalist has left, or until you are out of the recording studio. When you complete an interview for a publication you should say to the journalist that you are happy to take a call in the next few days if they need to check anything with you. This is because the best time to get corrections made to an article is before it lands on the editor's desk. The journalist will be less inclined to make changes once the editor has seen it.

If you have just taken part in a radio interview you might want to ask for a copy of the audio files to put on your website.

What to do if a media storm is gathering around you

The management guru Peter Drucker once joked that the first rule of corporate disasters is to find a scapegoat. The truth is that adverse media coverage happens to most companies at some point, as common as slump following boom. When it does happen you should bear the following in mind:

> ➤ Talk immediately with your lawyer about what you can and cannot say. Ask for a set of words that allows you to sound sympathetic without admitting liability.

> ➤ Get professional help regarding your company's image. It is cheaper than not getting professional help.

> ➤ Appoint one spokesperson for your organisation. This removes the chances of your staff making conflicting statements.

> ➤ Avoid the temptation to lie. The fact is you should not lie at any time when dealing with the media, but especially not if you are in trouble. Journalists have a nose for lies and will home in on any false statements.

> ➤ If a tragedy has occurred and your company has some connection to it you should avoid speculating on the cause. You should sympathise with any victims but leave speculation about causes to the relevant authorities.

> ➤ Try to avoid the phrase 'No comment'. It sounds a little inhumane and a little guilty.

PR agencies

A common question is should you do your own PR, or should you get an agency to do it for you? To answer this question we need to understand that PR boils down to three things:

➤ depth of knowledge of your company

➤ creativity

➤ contacts in the media.

The answer lies in whether your in-house team is better at these three things than the PR company you are thinking of engaging. Usually an in-house team will have a deeper knowledge of your company but their creative ideas are likely to dry up more quickly. As to the point about contacts in the media? Well, you should be wary of PR types who talk too freely about the number of contacts they have. You have to make a character judgement of those you meet.

Most large companies choose to outsource their PR. If you choose that route, you will want to know:

How to choose between PR agencies

There are five main ways to differentiate between PR agencies:

➤ You must know exactly what you want before you buy. This will quickly narrow your choices.

➤ You should be aware of a curious aspect of the PR industry, which is that most companies look to build clients for the long term but many PR firms do not. Some even seek to turn over clients as fast as possible. The issue to watch for is that your relationships with PR agencies can be like short-term holiday romances that promise the world through white-teethed smiles.

➤ PR companies are very good at presenting to you but you need to ignore the lights and glitter of their presentation. Instead, focus your attention on the staff who will be handling your account, and in particular on the team leader.

➤ The agency will only be able to perform for you if they act as part of your company. They have to know all about your company and they have to be all but a part of your company. Ask yourself how closely you can really work with these people.

➤ A successful PR operation will mean inordinate amounts of time and effort on your part because, just like salespeople, creative types need a lot more managing than the average employee. On the other hand, it is these two types – creatives and sales people – who have the most potential to offer your company. A good PR agency is as valuable as a second sales team.

New appointee letters

When PR companies run out of ideas they often suggest you send out press releases about new appointments in your company. It is an idea that works a lot better when you do it the other way round.

Specifically, you should read the new appointments features in the trade press and the *Financial Times*. You should then write to these people to congratulate them on their new appointment and to introduce your company. People taking up new positions are much more likely to read sales literature than old hands and they are more open to new ideas. This type of letter will catch them at the right time and in the right way.

Make the most of professional associations

An easy way to promote your company is to be listed in all the directories that are relevant to your trade or profession. Most of these are free to enter and they are a frequent starting point for buyers. The easiest way to find the relevant associations for your company is to look in an appropriate reference book. For example, the *Directory of British Associations*, published by CBD Research, is in most libraries and lists everything you need to know.

Win awards

Winning industry awards is another easy way to promote your company. There are approximately 18,000 awards in the UK and a number of them are very easy to win. (There is even an award ceremony for award ceremonies held at the Dorchester Hotel in London each December.) An award logo on your company-headed note paper will impress prospects. Here is how to win awards:

> The first step is obviously to choose the awards you want to win – those that would confer the most benefit on your company.

> Then you need to understand what is needed to win. Look at both the letter and the spirit of the rules.

> When you submit your entry you should give the judges a detailed plan of how you would publicise the win. They will look favourably on a candidate who plans to publicise the award.

> Look at how you can raise your profile with the judges. You do not want to be out of their sight or their mind.

> Invite the judges to see your people in action. It will make an impression.

However you sell, the chances are you will be using your skills in the face of the competition. So it is time we turned our focus to them ...

Chapter **14**

....

Tips on beating the competition

- What buyers are looking for
- Avoiding the biggest waste of a salesperson's time
- Four general rules for competitive situations
- Timing your visits when you are part of a formal bid process
- The waiting room

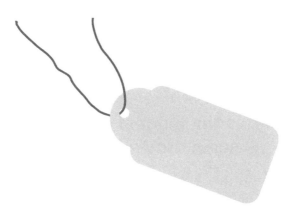

'Competition brings out the best in products and the worst in people.'

David Sarnoff (1891–1971), technology champion and corporate executive

If you want to beat the competition the place to do it is inside the buyer's mind.

What are the buyers looking for?

Actually, it is quite simple. Buyers are usually balancing just three factors when they make their decisions:

> Their primary concern is usually that they want a good quality product or service. For example, a well-written legal document or a well-built IT system.

> Their second concern is usually about time and cost.

> Their third concern is usually that they want to be seen, in the eyes of their colleagues and superiors, to have made a sensible choice of supplier. This is the origin of the phrase 'No one ever lost their job buying IBM'.

Whenever you face competition you should try and assess the value your prospect ascribes to each of these factors so that you can present what you offer accordingly. You will find that about 80 per cent of buyers place the three criteria in the order they are listed above.

However complex buying motives may at first appear, they will usually boil down to one or two issues that really matter to the prospect. It is very rare for there to be more than three. This rule applies to all sales, including the largest and most apparently complex.

There is one final point worth noting on this subject. Salespeople consistently believe that price is a more important factor than it actually is. The dangers here are not just about misdiagnosis. Over-focusing on price can lead the buyer to believe your company is offering something that is in some way lower quality.

So what is the biggest waste of a salesperson's time?

If you ask salespeople what constitutes the biggest waste of their time, the three most common answers you receive are:

> travelling

> admin and reporting

> gathering information on prospects.

Which answer would you choose?

Actually all the above answers are wrong. The biggest waste of sales-people's time is bidding for work that they do not win. It takes up about one-third of the average salesperson's time. Those salespeople would be a lot more efficient if they just walked away from the unwinnable sales at the beginning. From there on they are simply throwing good time after bad – and reinforcing their own failure.

The more respondents there are to a bid, the more important this rule becomes.

Bid fodder

By the time buyers gets to the stage of requesting bids they often have a good idea of the type of company they want to do the work. They may even have a particular company in mind but will still put the bid out to several companies. It may be that they want to bring competition to the bidding process or it may just be their policy to 'always get three quotes'. In situations like this the non-preferred companies are little more than bid fodder.

If another company has helped prepare the bid, the chances are that you are bid fodder. Consultancies are often involved in preparing bids and this gives them an inside track that is all but unbeatable. Indeed, a study by IBM concluded that in situations of this kind, the 'inside' consultancy wins the main piece of work over 80 per cent of the time.

When a bid comes up you need to use your intuition and gently probe this area with the prospect. There is little point asking 'Are we bid fodder?' but you can discreetly ask if they have had any outside help in preparing the bid.

But my boss tells me to go after everything

Why do so many directors insist that every bid is chased? Well, in some cases it is because the director is a compulsive over-gambler – a person who chases any opportunity, however long the odds. Anecdotal evidence from business psychologists suggests it is a more common trait in senior businesspeople than you might imagine.

Aside from this, there are usually three other reasons why directors insist on chasing every bid:

> First, company politics at director level takes place in a macho environment. In such an environment, a person advocating a 'bid for everything' policy wins political kudos, while the person

advocating selective bidding risks being labelled a wimp. That is a dangerous label because company politics, like all politics, rests more on belief than on fact.

➤ Second, when you are in the midst of a bid process, it can be difficult to take an objective view of your chances.

➤ The third reason is lack of other opportunities when there is pressure to perform. If your market looks to be a desert you will be tempted to grab at any green shoot you see.

If you genuinely think your company faces such a desert then you need to think about your situation and you need to be honest with yourself. It might genuinely be that your company works in an arid economic environment or it might be that your company has not searched hard enough for new business in the last two years. Once you know what the cause of the problem is you need to take action, because you cannot cross too many economic deserts. You only need your luck to run out once.

Four general rules for competitive situations

1 RULE ONE: Know your enemy

If you know nothing about your competitors you will win about a third of the work you bid for. (More on this in the next chapter.) If you know the competition as well as you know your own company you will win about 80 per cent of the work. The reason is that if you know the strengths and weaknesses of your competition it is very easy to work out what they will do in each situation.

Therefore you should ask the prospect about the competition because some prospects will name them if you but ask. Even if they will not name the competitors, most will tell you the *type* of competition you face. This information is also worth having.

Much like your information for bids you should have a central place for people to deposit any information they have about the competition.

You can sometimes glean information on competitors from the documents the prospect sends you. Whenever you receive such an electronic document from a prospect you should click on File, then Properties. This will tell you a great deal about the docu-ment. Of course the sender can hide this information if they choose but very few people are aware of the feature.

2 **RULE TWO:** Portray your company as a specialist

In most areas of human activity, specialists do better work than generalists. Most buyers will know or sense this.

3 **RULE THREE:** Don't knock the competition

Well, not in plain daylight anyway, because that will reflect badly on you. The best way to expose a competitor's weakness is to ensure the prospect finds the weakness 'themselves'. You can do this by directing the prospect's thoughts to areas where you are strong and the competition is weak.

Alternatively, you can invite your prospect to visit client sites that highlight your strengths and the competitor's weaknesses. The conversation that takes place there between your clients and your prospects will do your work for you.

4 **RULE FOUR:** Be nicer than the competition

We already know that people do not buy from companies but from people. This is particularly important when the prospect's character is people-oriented rather than task-oriented. Being nicer than the next person is a big factor in winning service sales but most people considerably underestimate its value.

Timing your visits when you are part of a formal bid process

Many bids follow formal processes. You are presented with a choice of times at which you meet the buying committee and another choice of times at which you present. In both cases you should always ask for the last time slot. Here is why:

> The actual process of talking to suppliers helps the buyer refine their needs. Therefore the supplier in the last time slot will get the most accurate definition of those needs.

> ➤ Buyers tend to become more open with each potential supplier they see. It is just human nature. They will be at their most open by the time they get to the last time slot.

> ➤ In the later time slots buyers often touch on the discussions they had with earlier bidders. Hearing about these discussions can only help you.

There is only one exception to this rule in that you should not ask for the last time slot if it falls late on a Friday afternoon. Every minute past 5.00 p.m. on a Friday that you spend with a prospect does more harm than good. They just want to get home.

The waiting room

In most bid processes there is a period between the date at which the bids must be in and the date at which the winner is announced. It is often called the 'waiting room' and is a period when time seems to hang in the air. It is a nervous time for you – having to wait for a decision you can no longer influence. During this period, contacts between the seller and buyer can be formalised and may even be prohibited.

But you need to think of the buyer's situation at this stage. It is a nervous time for them too, because they have to make a decision. You can use that nervousness to your advantage. Every bidder left in the last round can do the job. The buyer's decision will be coloured by emotion and any influence you can exert at this time will be particularly effective.

It is also at this time that the buyer will give you clues to your progress. The words they use and the amount of time they spend with you will probably tell you what they are thinking. There will usually be enough clues to their thoughts, but the trick is to interpret them correctly.

The solution to the waiting room is this. Early on in the sales process you should make arrangements for the buyer to visit one of your customers and the timing of that visit should coincide with the waiting-room period. Meeting one of your clients at a time when the buyer is under pressure will make the buyer feel assured. They will gain a feeling of comfort and trust in your company at a critical time. If you cannot arrange a site visit, try for a telephone reference instead.

Once you are consistently beating the competition you will want to trumpet your success. To do that you will need to measure your performance ...

Chapter **15**

··

How to measure performance

- Measuring your performance against the competition
- Measuring your own performance
- Your real chances of winning the work
- Sales reporting
- Rewarding sales achievement

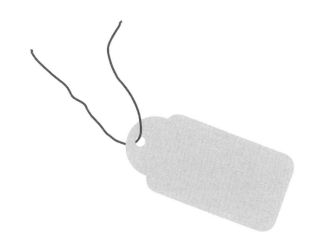

'I am only as good as my last battle.'

Napoleon Bonaparte (1769–1821), emperor

Measuring your performance against the competition

A good rule of thumb for selling is that you will win about one-third of the work you quote for. (A 'quote' here means either written quotes or precise verbal quotes.) This rule has obvious uses for predicting your company's sales. Broadly, it means that your monthly pipeline of potential services work should contain about two-and-a-half times the amount of work you could actually do. If you win a third of that pipeline you will be running at about 80 per cent billable time for your staff, which is about the rate most service companies target. The pipeline for product sales should be nearer three times.

This rule is also useful for analysing your sales performance. If you consistently win less than one-third of your quotes there is probably room for improvement in your proposal writing. If your win rate is in the 40+ per cent bracket then you need to be honest with yourself as to why that is. For example, it might be that you are unusually good at the later stages of the sales process or, more likely, it might be that you are concentrating too much on established clients.

Measuring your own performance

Salespeople predicting their future sales tend to overestimate their chances of winning by about 25–30 per cent. Therefore they should not be the ones doing the pipeline analysis. The team manager is a better choice for that.

What are the real chances of winning the work?

These percentages will give you a more objective view of your chances:

5 per cent	You have identified a specific opportunity with a prospect.
20 per cent	You have identified a specific opportunity with a customer.
33 per cent	You have submitted a written proposal.
50 per cent	You have submitted a written proposal and the prospect is keen to see you.
90 per cent	The prospect has verbally awarded the contract to you.
25 per cent	The verbal award was more than two months ago but you have not started the work yet.

Sales reporting

How frequently should you report on performance?

The more junior a salesperson, the more frequent should be their reporting. However, reporting for senior salespeople is best done on a monthly basis. This is because the act of reporting takes up valuable sales time in itself. Also, monthly reporting gives a clearer picture than any other frequency.

Daily reporting for senior salespeople can be very damaging to a sales team's morale. People responsible for implementing these regimes nearly all gave variations on the same, rather ironic, answer. Namely that daily reporting was brought in to tackle a sales crisis.

What should the sales report look like?

Here is an example of a typical monthly report:

FIGURE 1

Monthly sales report: Laura Reddy, December

1 New orders and follow-on work won this month

Bid or project name	Client	New or existing?	Value	Expected start and end months	Description
	Lantro Pharma	Existing	£75,000	January	Security work
Total			**£75,000**		

2 Bids lost, gone away or not bidded

Bid or project name	Client	Value	Description (lost/gone away/not bidded)/Reason
	Ganymede Financial Services Ltd	£50,000	Work lost to Holistic Paradigms Consulting
	Cusack Research	£185,000	Declined to bid – we have no realistic chance of winning
Total		**£235,000**	

3 Bids and prospects summary: qualified prospects and bids in preparation or submitted

Bid or project name	Client	New or existing?	Month bid submitted	Value	Probability	Weighted	Month decision due	Expected start and end months	Description
	The Making Difference Company	New	October	£150,000	50 per cent	£75,000	January	February to March	Help with innovative ways of doing things
	Ontario Sapphire Inc.	New	November	£100,000	33 per cent	£36,300	January	February to June	Supply of networking products
	Gooster Publishing, Ireland	New	October	£250,000	50 per cent	£125,000	Decision imminent	Would all be paid in December	See section 7 of this report
Total				**£500,000**		**£236,300**			

Note: You might want to add additional columns to highlight whether the work is fixed price or time and materials. You might also want to include a column on profitability.

4 Suspects

Bid or project name	Client	Approx. Value	Date bid likely to be submitted	Date work likely to start	Description (including next steps)
	TT-Ratio GmbH	Unknown	February	Unknown	Installation of financial product
Total					

5 Meetings arranged for next month

Client/name/position	Existing work or new opportunity?	Objectives
Auckland Imaging	New	Aiming to break into new account
Clarity Telecom Co.	Existing	Possible texting services opportunity

Note: You might want to alter section 5 to show both the meetings you had in this month and those you plan for next month.

6 Progress against annual targets

Target	Sold so far	Booked revenue	Remainder
2,000,000	1,500,000	300,000	200,000

7 Action plan

If I can win the Gooster Publishing deal I can hit my target.

8 Any other business

How should you reward sales achievement?

There are three golden rules to designing a good sales reward scheme:

> Sales teams paid commission outsell those on straight salaries.

> The simpler the commission scheme the more is sold.

> Commission schemes can be used to steer a sales team with absolute precision. One tweak to these schemes can change the course of the largest companies.

Of course that all begs the question as to what makes the best commission scheme. It depends on your industry sector, but for new business the following holds good. The sales person, on winning the new account, is paid about 2 per cent of its value in the first year and 1 per cent in the second. In the third year the management of the account, and the earnings from it, revert to an account management team.

Bringing order to your measurement will certainly help your sales but it will never be a battle winner in its own right. There is, however, one area of sales where order is definitely a battle winner ...

Chapter **16**

Tips on managing your contacts

- Why you need a contact management system
- How to choose the right one

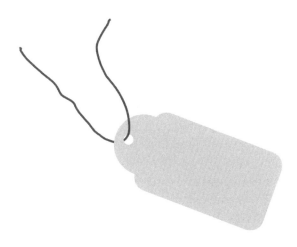

'It takes less to keep an old customer satisfied than it takes to get a new customer interested.'

Richard Denny, author

Why do you need a contact management system?

An analogy about forests and villages might seem a little out of place here, but please bear with me while I explain it. During the Middle Ages most of Europe was forest, which was gradually cleared to make into farmland. The fertility of the cleared land would gradually deteriorate and so a bit more of the surrounding forest would need to be cleared. Your existing client base will gradually lose its profitability in the way farmland loses its fertility. And so you need a regular supply of new customers to compensate for this. A good contact management system gives you the capability to farm your known contacts in the most efficient way possible. It also allows you to maximise the time you spend on forest clearing and to do that job efficiently.

Most people know that the company's most valuable asset is its staff. However, far fewer can correctly name the second most valuable asset. It is the customers and the prospects. The best way to look after this second asset is to use a contact management system.

So much for the theory. The reality is that people will only use a contact management system if they believe it will help them personally. Systems that are seen as just another piece of admin or another chore are certain to fail. In a moment we will look at the specific features you need in a contact management system, but first we should look at why you should have one.

What have you got to gain from such a system?

> **Improved knowledge of your market, and your company's position in that market.** A good system allows you to maintain good quality relationships with a large part of your target audience. This is a valuable and simple thing to do and the chances are that your competitors do not do it well.

> **More efficient sales and marketing.** Such a system increases the number of meetings you set up and the number of attendees you get to your seminars. The biggest single cost for seminars is the cost of getting people to attend. A good list – one made of good quality contacts – removes that cost. It also allows you to send regular, meaningful e-mailshots and makes your company more customer-oriented.

> **Building something of lasting value.** Lots of sales teams live from one month to the next. Once you are confident that your system

holds a high percentage of your target contacts, you will have built something of long-term value. This long-term outlook will help sustain you through the adversities of selling and will help you avoid a month-by-month existence. You can safely spend less on renting and buying lists from outside sources.

> **A better spread of your company's risks.** Most firms rely too much on a handful of clients and may have 80 per cent of their work coming from 20 per cent of their clients. Think what would happen to your company if it lost its two largest clients over the next six months. If that prospect fills you with horror, then your company probably needs to spread its sales risks.

> **Improved retention of information.** A contact system means detailed records of customers reside in one central place, in the company's ownership. This is probably a big advance on your company's current situation, as most companies have customer records, with mixed levels of detail, in several different places. When someone leaves, much of that person's knowledge goes with them – an astonishing way to handle a company's second most valuable asset.

It is often the case in sales that just staying in the chase is enough to win. The competition may well be tracking the opportunity you are tracking, but over six or twelve months most of them will drop out. Here is another analogy to prove this point. The most primitive type of hunting is that practised by the San Bushmen of the Kalahari. They know that over a 24-hour period a human can cover a greater distance than any four-legged animal because running on two legs is much more energy-efficient than running on four. The Bushmen keep jogging for that length of time, keeping the animal in sight, and knowing that the animal will need to stop before they do. When that happens the animal is theirs for the taking. You will often find that you can win a sale just by keeping in contact with the opportunity until the time comes for you to simply walk in and win it.

> **Nurturing the sales abilities of your staff.** Your staff's confidence in their sales ability will grow in proportion to the number of good quality contact names they put in the system. They will enjoy the feeling of building something valuable and they will have a clear view of how their individual actions add to the company's achievements.

On top of that a good system will also allow you to develop your own forest clearers, who are a valuable asset to any company.

Which names do you want in this system?

To be successful, most companies only need to have relationships with a small number of people in the whole country – rarely more than a thousand. Perhaps you think this number is too low? Well, your company probably focuses its sales efforts on the largest 500 companies or outlets in the country. How many people in those 500 targets companies actually make decisions about contracts or purchases in your particular specialisation? Is it 10, 20? It is very unlikely to be more. (The situation is very similar to that faced by our sewing machine salesman on page 73.)

If you develop good relationships with those few thousand key people, then before long your contact system will be full of high-grade contacts.

Those few thousand contacts divide into three groups:

➢ existing clients

➢ past clients

➢ prospects.

Known contacts and past contacts are nearly always 'warm' towards your company. Prospects will be 'cold' when you first contact them but warm thereafter. Keeping in contact with them every few months means that, when they have needs, you will know about them. And you will probably be their preferred choice of supplier for the work.

So where are the hidden contacts to put in your system?

Good places to look are:

➢ the past customers list

➢ the 'contacts' section in your staff's e-mail program

➢ business cards collected by your staff

➢ the lists of people who attended your seminars

➢ the prospect lists you bought over time.

To populate the system you should start by putting in these contacts. The chances are that they alone will cover a reasonable percentage of your target market, and keeping those names up to date will cover still more of it.

You might then choose to go one step further. If you want to have all your target market in the system you can put in the head office and switchboard details for those companies that are target companies but for whom you do not have any contacts. A mailshot from such a system would then reach a lot of the people you would want to reach.

Choosing a contact management system

You need a good contacts system, but how do you choose something appropriate? What you should not do is search the web for three such systems and then invite salespeople from those companies to demonstrate their products. All that will happen is that the salespeople will mould your 'needs' to fit the features of their particular products and you will probably end up buying from the best salesperson. It is much like visiting that fictional doctor who offers the same pill for every ailment.

A better starting point is to spend time developing a clear idea of what you need from the system. Many people in this situation decide that what they want is 'the best tool on the market' but what they actually want is the one that best fits their needs.

So what functionality do you actually need for a contact management system? Well, there are five key rules:

> **Keep the functionality to the absolute minimum.** Whatever the salesperson tells you, you do not need the additional functionality. It just confuses things.

> **All the information should appear on one screen.** The people who use the system simply will not check for information on hidden screens.

> **Only flat-file structures work.** Regardless of how the information is stored in the database, the users should be presented with a flat-file structure. (Flat-file structures are also known as 'card index' structures.) The salesperson might tell you that most computer databases have a relational structure to store information. That is certainly true and a relational structure is the best way for a computer to store information. The point is that while the computer stores it that way it will have no problem presenting it in a flat-file structure, and that is the best way for the users to view it.

> **Choose technology platforms that are industry standards.** Technical obsolescence is a big problem for IT products and you do not want to be choosing another new system in a few years' time.

> **Make sure everyone wants to use it.** The key to success with these systems is to get the whole company to buy in. You will need to sell it internally.

So which system should you go for?

It could take a lot of your time to compile a list of the functionality you need, so here is a list to save you doing that.

The top half of the screen should have:

> the company name

> the contact name

> their address

> the switchboard number

> their direct line number

> their mobile number

> their PA's name

> their e-mail address

> a tick box that denotes which of your company offices has responsibility for them

> a tick box that denotes the prospects who should only be contacted by letter or e-mail, not by telephone

> a note of the next date on which the contact should be called

> the name of the person from your company who handles the account

> the original source of the lead

> the prospect's industry sector, e.g. government, finance, industry etc.

> their job title

> the function they work in – i.e. central buying, finance, marketing etc.

> the level of influence they have: it is best to keep this at two levels – either a key decision maker (KDM) or an influencer

> a tick box to say whether they should receive a Christmas card from your company

> their birthday, if you know it – it is worth sending your customers birthday cards (but not your prospects as that would be inappropriate).

> the bottom half of the screen should scroll. This allows your staff to write a succinct note of each conversation they have with a prospect. (An automatic date stamp function is useful here, as is an automatic user ID stamp.)

> the system data should also have the ability to attach documents to your notes so that you can refer back to them easily.

FIGURE 1

Example contact screen

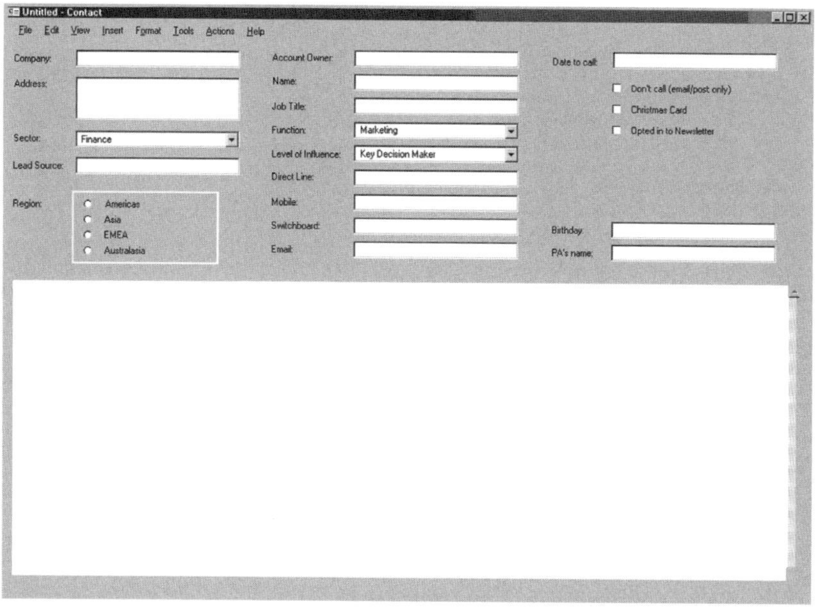

Over time, some of the accounts in your contact system will flourish and prosper. To develop them further, you will need different techniques ...

Chapter **17**

Tips on managing large accounts

- How to network around an account
- How to get extra work from the account
- Shaping the strategy of their senior managers
- When a team runs the account

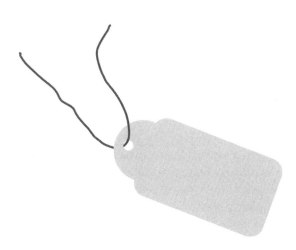

'It is not always by plugging away at a difficulty and sticking at it that one overcomes it. Certain people, and certain things, require to be approached from an angle.'

Matthew Arnold (1822–88), poet

Increasingly, companies buy on national, regional or global levels. When that happens they often stipulate that their suppliers provide uniform levels of price and service in every location. This is exactly the type of account you are looking for, but how should you go about managing it? The first step is ...

Get more background information on the company

Generally, the larger the company, the easier it is to find information about it. As we saw earlier, the directors' statement at the front of the company's annual report will usually tell you a lot of what you need to know. Even the largest companies will only have a few issues. And the larger the company, the more completely its issues will be in the public domain.

Once you know the issues the next thing you will want is an organisational chart. Ideally you should have notes for each of the people on the chart. (How you do that is up to you, but a click-through link, much like the internet, is a popular solution.)

Charts detailing the senior international directors look good but are only useful if you actually sell at that level. Information about people lower down the chain is not so readily available but is probably more valuable.

So how do you network around the account?

Most people are delighted when they are first appointed to look after a strategic account. Not least because existing clients return roughly four times as much work in the first year as new clients. However, once in the role, you often find that the account's 'strategic' status actually rests on a handful of relationships, some of which are weak.

Focusing on those few established relationships you inherit is comforting, but some of those people will move jobs and others will simply run out of work to give you. Not all cleared land stays fertile forever, so you need to develop new relationships in the account. Here is how to do that.

Assess the value of the relationships you already have

A good way to start is to classify each contact. Most of your contacts will fall comfortably into one of the following five categories:

FIGURE 1

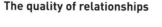

The quality of relationships

Trusted referee

Customer

Prospect

Suspect

In-target market

The more people you can get as trusted referees the more durable the account becomes. Here is how to go about that.

Get help from the people you already know in the account

Of course the big advantage you have with an existing account is that you have existing contacts. These people can help you in three main ways:

> ➤ The chances are that at least one of them will be able to supply you with some sort of organisational chart.

> ➤ Once you have such a chart, other contacts within the account will add names to it. Some of them will also point out where the opportunities lie.

> ➤ Others will probably agree to act as referees for you. People are much quicker to talk to referees within their own company and they tend to be more believing of them.

Write a one-page summary of the work you have done in that account

This can be quite simple – just a summary of what you have done for that client and an outline of any pre-existing agreements you have with them. E-mailing this to other people in that account will get you a lot of new meetings.

Ways to get extra work from these contacts

Organise some events specifically for that company

Specifically, these are hotel away-days of the sort mentioned in Chapter 12. For example, you can host a day at a country hotel for a group of managers to discuss their company's strategy in a particular area. This will throw up lots of opportunities for you.

Wheel in your big guns

Accounts grow better when the personal success of a senior figure in your company is tied to the growth of that account. A good way to arrange this is for you and a close contact from the account to arrange a meeting between a senior figure from your company and a senior figure from their company. Most senior people expect a briefing document when such a meeting is being prepared and that is something you and your contact can sit down and prepare together. Delegating upwards has all manner of benefits.

Recognise opportunities

You will not always have to make your own opportunities when managing accounts. Some will be all but handed to you. The most likely times for this to happen are:

> industry or market changes

> mergers and acquisitions

> client requests for help with changing their business

> changes in key staff.

You just have to capitalise on these events.

When a team runs the account

Keep everyone from your company who is involved with the account informed of events. The best way to do this is to issue a monthly account summary. It need not be complex. The following format will cover everything.

FIGURE 2

Monthly account summary

Account name
Financial status of the account
Achievements last month ➤ ➤ ➤
Planned achievements this month ➤ ➤ ➤
Outstanding commercial issues ➤ ➤ ➤
Outstanding technical/supply issues ➤ ➤ ➤

The larger your accounts become, the more you will find yourself involved in negotiations. So it is time to look at that.

Chapter **18**

Tips on negotiation

- Five questions that will prepare your negotiation position
- Nine rules for the actual negotiations
- Group negotiation
- Common situations when negotiating
- How professional buyers buy

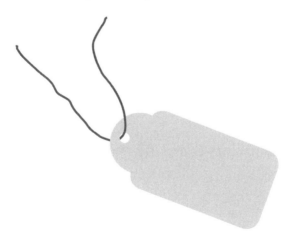

'*Seek first to understand, then to be understood.*'

Stephen Covey (b. 1932), business writer

We should begin with the cardinal rule of negotiation ...

If you can avoid negotiating, do

Because the strongest agreements are more usually reached by consensus, than by conflict. Negotiations can consume a lot of time, money and goodwill.

Prospects frequently ask questions that are invitations to negotiate and the trick to responding is to avoid getting dragged into the detail. This is because the process of breaking down your service into its constituent parts tends to destroy the value of the whole package you are offering. Therefore when you are asked this type of question you should frame your answer to refer back to the value of the *whole* package you offer.

There will, of course, be situations in which negotiation is unavoidable. This chapter is about those situations.

Five questions that will prepare your negotiation position

Few things in life benefit more from preparation than negotiation. The bulk of that preparation is about considering your interests and those of your opposite number. You will be able to deduce what most of their interests must be. Once you have done that you need to think about the tradables.

1 So what exactly are the tradables?

A tradable is a fluid part of the negotiations – something that can be readily swapped between the two parties in the deal. They can often be swapped in many ingenious ways before the deal is finally agreed. Before the meeting, you should work out what all the tradables are. A good way to do that is to draw up a grid like this:

FIGURE 1

	Tradables	Non-tradables
Seller	Availability of juniors Day rates of consultants Location of work	Availability of Partners Warranties
Buyer	Capital outlay or ongoing cost Choice of supplier Provision of case studies	Completion date Quality of end product Their manager's view of their performance

This covers all the key tradables when selling services. Product sales have a lot more. For example, the myriad tariffs available when you buy a mobile phone, or all the extras you can have with a new piece of IT equipment. However, exactly the same principles apply because the prospect's focus will only ever be on a few of the options. They are what the negotiation will be about.

2 What is the value of each tradable to each party?

You and the prospect will not attach the same value to each tradable and that is where much of the negotiation lies. Therefore you should think about the value of each tradable to each party so that when it comes to the meeting you will be able to swap and alter each one and so get the best match for both sides.

It helps to give a value to each tradable on a scale of one to ten, because then you will be able to hold on to a fixed value for things through the swirling mêlée of bargaining. More complexity is added in situations where the value of two tradables together is worth more than their value when separate.

If your character is one that is eager to please others, then this part of the preparation is particularly important because such a temperament can easily give away too much in negotiation.

3 Along what path is the conversation likely to develop?

The more you think about the prospect's situation the stronger you will be. That means you should go over the conversation beforehand – either in your head or on paper.

4 Where should you pitch your opening offer?

First you need to think about where the middle ground between you and your opposite number is likely to be. Once you have done that you will want to pitch your starting position some way past the mid-point to give yourself negotiation room. In western culture that pitch should be about 20 per cent past the mid-point – more if your adversary is particularly combative.

5 What is your fall-back position?

'Fall-back position' means the line that marks the minimum you are prepared to accept; the point after which you would be better off not agreeing a deal. The dangers of not preparing a fall-back position are twofold:

➤ You will have less idea of what constitutes a good or bad outcome.

➤ You are more likely to lose a negotiation if you do not start with any fixed points.

If you do not know your fall-back position before you enter the negotiations you will spend a lot of the time negotiating with yourself as to what you are prepared to accept.

Nine rules for the actual negotiations

1 Uncover their true interests

Your first task is to check you understand what the other party is *really* about because people frequently start negotiations by taking a position that is not a true statement of their situation. For this reason, you should not immediately try to tackle a position head-on. Rather, it is better to sidestep the position while you ask questions that uncover their true interests. Bill Clinton has a reputation for being particularly adept at this and it is a real key to success in negotiations. The truth is you cannot resolve a negotiation successfully until you have got to the core of the other party's situation.

People take false positions for one of two reasons:

> They have not thought through their situation properly.
> They are deliberately trying to hide something.

Usually, they have not thought through their situation. When that happens you will be at an advantage. Alternatively, if they have taken up a false position because they are hiding something, it means they have been thinking like a politician. In brief, before a politician takes a position on an issue, they assess the various influences on the situation and then choose the position that most suits their self-interest. They then dress that position in moral clothes for public consumption. If you sense that the other party has done that, then you can usually work out their true interests by working backwards from the position they have taken.

The best way to judge the intentions of another person is to use a mixture of logic, reason and intuition. Be aware that intuition is not quite the same thing as emotion, which leads us on to the second rule ...

2 Do not let emotion colour your thoughts

Emotion has little to contribute to negotiating. The trouble with it is that in negotiation we tend to use emotion to judge the motives of others, and, in the absence of knowledge, we tend to assume their motives are to do us down. For most of us, the more important the issue, the more emotion colours our fears. It is very human to think like this. The fact is, most human disagreements are caused not by malice, but by misunderstanding.

There is just one area where emotion can help you in negotiation ...

3 You should describe your situation with emotion and colour

This part should all but overflow with emotion, colour and human interest – as much as is credible in the circumstances. Doing so will have two effects:

> It will help persuade the other party that you are being truthful, and that will help them trust you.
> A powerful speech, delivered from the heart, will sway them some way towards your viewpoint.

Done properly this negotiating technique can be highly persuasive.

4 But keep the people and the subject separate

People often fear that 'hard' negotiation will damage the relationship they have with the other party. Well, it will be damaging if the other party perceives it to be a personal attack. It is unlikely to be damaging if they think you are just focusing on the subject matter.

5 Do not give away something for nothing

When negotiating, you need to adopt the mindset that everything has a value and that nothing should be given away for free. You need to assign objective values to what you are trading, including intangible assets such as client goodwill and trust.

6 Do not accept their first offer

Because you will almost certainly get a better offer if you haggle. The main exception to this rule is when people approach these conversations in the manner of an open consultation rather than a negotiation. In these situations a hard-line negotiation style will be to your short-term gain but your long-term loss. The reason is that, over time, the other party will grow to think less of you if you consistently negotiate like that. It is another reason why you should avoid negotiation if you possibly can.

Of course, the other time to accept their first offer is when that offer is close to what you are looking for.

7 Make sure you cover everything, and are reasonably fair

Deals that overwhelmingly favour one party tend not to last. The best negotiations are those that favour you, but not too much.

8 Keep your own counsel

In most negotiations the person who talks most gives most away. Another reason why you should use your ears twice as much as your mouth.

9 Organise group negotiations

At times, this will feel like organising synchronised swimming for cats. However, there will be times when you cannot avoid organising group negotiations. The best tactic for these situations is to have one of your team as the lead speaker and another whose role is just to listen. The senior figure should be the speaker and the most intuitive should be the listener.

The most common negotiation situations

The other party keeps asking for a discount

Whenever they do this you should ask them what their *core* reason is for wanting that discount. For example, a prospect saying 'It's too expensive' can mean several different things and you need to discover what they really mean by it. It usually means one of the following:

> They genuinely think that the price is too high.

> They are just 'trying it on' – hoping for a price cut.

> As a matter of pride they will only employ someone if they can drive a deal from them.

We already know that when price is an objection you should not tackle it until all the other objections have been sorted. If you have reached that position then the basics of the answers you should adopt to each of these possible situations are as follows:

They genuinely think the price is too high In this instance you need to define their question – the price is too high in comparison with what? Their expectations? The value that would come from it? The competitor's price? Once you have got to the core of this objection you can usually solve it.

They are 'trying it on' – hoping for a price cut Here it is best to stand your ground politely and firmly. However, there are two things to have in mind when doing this:

> You will need to be polite and humble – if they do not get a concession their ego is likely to be bruised and you need to be aware of that. You should make it easy for them to back down by being humble in victory.

> You should ask yourself if there is a danger behind the question. Can the competition still come back if you do not offer a price cut? Most prospects will not change suppliers for a small price advantage but you must keep an eye to it.

As a matter of pride they will only employ someone if they can drive a deal from them In these instances you should look for a solution that salves their 'honour' but gives away little of substance.

Other common situations in negotiation are:

You need to stand your ground

The best way to stand your ground is to politely refer back to the value for money you offer and the quality of what you offer. When the prospect talks about cost, you should talk about value.

During this part of the negotiation it is tempting to say something like 'I'm making a generous offer'. And you may well be. The point is justification statements like that will do nothing to help your cause because they are always seen by the other party as arrogant and antagonistic. A salesperson's job is not to antagonise, but to persuade. Therefore any self-justification statement needs to be rephrased to focus on the benefits of your offer.

You need to give ground

The trick to giving ground, and the trick to reducing your price, is to do so in small amounts. For example, if you need to lower your price you should not lower it with numbers that end in nought or five. Using the other numbers will make it harder for the other party to push for large reductions without appearing unreasonable.

You need to expand the playing field

If one side wins in negotiation, it does not mean that the other side must lose. Often there is scope to be creative and to agree a situation where both sides win. This type of agreement often means a third party loses. For example, when politicians are faced with an apparently zero-sum game they often expand the playing field. (Most commonly by placing the burden on the environment, or on future tax revenues.)

It is getting a bit heated

The best negotiations are conducted in atmospheres of mutual benefit, but inevitably some degenerate into a trading of veiled threats. When this happens, you should either hold back, or deliver one huge knockout blow. US President Roosevelt summed this up when he said 'Don't hit at all if it's honourably possible to avoid hitting; but never hit softly'. As with so many forms of persuasion one big reason is a lot more compelling than several small ones.

There is just one more thing to know ...

How do professional buyers buy?

The most common tactic they use is the following. Once they have whittled the field down to three bidders they will rank them in their own mind as first, second and third choice. Therefore the buyer already knows they will buy from bidder one but starts by approaching the bidder ranked third. The buyer then suggests to that bidder that they are interested in buying but has a problem with the price. The effect of this will be to drive down the price offered by that bidder. Armed with that information the buyer then goes on to the second placed bidder and does the same thing again, so reducing the price still further. Finally, armed with that quote, the buyer talks with the bidder they intend to choose. Of course, what the buyer has done here is leave price until it is the only remaining issue.

That covers all the main points about negotiation. You will find that your toughest negotiations won't be with prospects or customers. They will be with lawyers. So how do you deal with them?

Chapter **19**

··

How to sort the contracts stage painlessly

- What you need in a heads of agreement
- Some general considerations for contracts
- Tips for dealing with lawyers
- Frequently occurring problems with commercial contracts
- Getting the legal side right in the real world

'Diplomacy is the art of telling plain truth without giving offence.'

Winston Churchill (1874–1965), statesman

There are two main reasons for agreeing contracts. One is to protect your interests. The other is to make things clear.

This chapter shows you how to tie up the legal side of things. If you are a non-lawyer you may not be enthusiastic about this part of selling, but it is a part of the sale that needs to be done properly at the time if problems are not to appear later.

A newly agreed deal is a precarious thing that may need nurturing to survive. A few days after the deal is first struck, issues often surface on which the two parties cannot agree. And when that happens it is all too easy for one party to walk away. You can dramatically reduce the chances of this happening if, when the sale is verbally agreed, you and the other party draft a written heads of agreement. This is a document that describes the key features of the work in plain English rather than legal language. Once you and the prospect have a heads of agreement, then is the time to hand it to your lawyer. They will take out the punctuation for you, and put random words into Latin.

Most work falls into two main types:

> One-off pieces of work such as a legal case, or developing an IT product for a specific customer.

> Ongoing work. This is open-ended work, such as an agreement to supply a set number of staff hours each month, or a set number of items each month.

The heads of agreement for both types of contract will have much in common.

What should be in the heads of agreement?

The following is a stage 1 for a heads of agreement, which will cover 90 per cent of your work.

1 Contact details for each party

You will need the names, addresses and contact details for key figures from each party – your company and theirs. Typically this will be the project manager or the project owner from each side. You will also want something for situations in which higher authority is needed on either side.

2 A description of the deal

Here you should insert a reasonably detailed project plan, or an agreement about levels of service and delivery. You should describe the deal in plain English.

3 A set of timescales

All projects need them. You need to think about what exactly it is you want to commit to. (You will need to commit to something.) Most commonly, it will be a set of deliverables, a set of timescales, or an acceptance process.

4 Something about the money

This usually means sorting two things: the fee rates and the payment schedules.

5 Confidentiality clause

Prospects usually ask for such clauses because they fear that their hard work and innovation might be copied cheaply by the competition. If this happens to you, you will probably have no choice but to accept. You need to choose your time to talk about confidentiality clauses because they can inadvertently rule out the writing of case studies and case studies are something you want.

6 Security

Many prospects have concerns, very understandably, about security. You should handle the client's security concerns in a warm and human way because this is an area where you have little to lose and a lot to win.

7 Non-solicitation clauses

These are clauses that preclude the parties from poaching each other's staff. You need to decide before the meeting whether you want this clause to restrict or protect you. The maximum non-solicitation period you can reasonably expect when a contract finishes is six months. (UK courts will only rarely enforce a longer period, even if there is a written contract between the two parties to that effect.)

The need for these clauses is often queried because your staff will have signed something very similar when they joined your company. However, when one of your staff does try to change their employment status to work directly for the client, you will find that they are nearly always allowed to do so because the client is seen as 'too important to annoy'. Having a non-solicitation agreement with a client will greatly reduce the chances of this happening because it sets expectations from the outset.

8 An agreement on intellectual property

This is a topic in its own right and is detailed later in this chapter.

9 An agreed way to correct problems

Agreeing this before the work starts will save you a lot of future stress.

10 A limitation of the liabilities

The wording of these clauses is best left to lawyers. You just need to agree the general principles. To get to those principles you need to think about what would happen if there was a breach of contract by your company. When that happens, two things tend to be important:

- ➤ Have you limited your liability to a fixed sum? Damages are often limited to the value of the contract. Is that a suitable value for you and the other party?

- ➤ Does your company have suitable professional indemnity insurance?

11 The termination provisions

When is the natural end for the work? If you are doing a one-off project or fulfilling a one-off order the answer will be obvious. Deals that involve an open-ended supply of staff or products are rather different. Most notice periods state that either party can give notice at any time and then just work the notice period. But there are other ways to define notice periods and you should try to choose one that suits you best.

For example, a better agreement, from your point of view, would be one in which the buyer can only give notice on the anniversary of the contract's signing, i.e. on one day per year. The practical effects of such an agreement are that your contracts are likely to last longer and you will get a year's warning of any changes.

12 Ancillary services

This is rarely discussed when people are talking about heads of agreement but it is an excellent way to cement what you do for the client. Typically, ancillary services means things such as training, support, facilities management and so on.

13 What type of contract do you want?

Finally, you should decide whether the contract is time and materials, fixed price or capped. Time and materials means you just supply staff or products. Fixed price means you agree to do a piece of work to set criteria for a set cost. The real difference between the two is about which party pays in the event of extra work needing to be done. Capped contracts are of course a hybrid of the two and they can be the least efficient way of doing things (they are most common in government contracts).

Some general points about contracts

Be wary of lawyers

You should never agree a document with a prospect's lawyer until a lawyer from your side has seen it. The document may seem fair and clear to you but some words have subtly different meanings when used by lawyers and many of those differences are legally defined. As Shakespeare put it, 'the devil can cite scripture for his purpose'. Since he penned those words lawyers have been busy doing just that.

Here is a list of the more common tricks you should be familiar with:

> The other party's lawyer may ask you to agree that, in the event of a fault in your company's work, you make 'all reasonable efforts' to resolve it, rather than just making 'reasonable efforts.' There is a world of difference in the legal meaning of these two phrases. 'Reasonable efforts' broadly means that you need to be prompt about fixing the issue, but you are not expected to tear your company apart to achieve the result. 'All reasonable efforts' broadly means that your company has to commit whatever resources it takes to fix the problem and those resources need to be committed immediately. It is the sort of phrase that can sink your company.

> Another common example is the legal meaning of the word 'procure'. If you see it in a contract it does not mean you have to obtain something. It means you are guaranteeing something.

> Another common trick is to put deliberate spelling mistakes into the contract. For example, there is little difference between 'contractor' and 'contractee' when the two words are surrounded by a forest of legal language. The difference in meaning is, of course, immense.

You may feel a little cynical about lawyers and the core of the problem is that justice is a human invention rather than something that occurs in nature. That means that morality and the law are only loosely related. Cousins but not siblings. And justice is rarely better than those who dispense it.

Do not leave lawyers together for too long

It is common thing for two parties to agree a deal and leave the details to be sorted by their respective lawyers. The lawyers then come back at some later date citing 'irreconcilable' reasons why the deal cannot be agreed. If you do not keep a close eye on your affairs there is many a lawyer who will untie what you so carefully wove. They will tell you they do not kill deals, but they are often in attendance when the patient expires.

What do intellectual property rights (IPR) mean in plain language?

IPR are commonly disputed in contracts so it is worth summarising the main points. This is not so daunting when you realise that, even in the higher courts, IPR disputes usually boil down to just two things:

> Who owns the IPR of the *end product*.

> Who owns the IPR of the *method used* to make the end product.

The *end product* delivered by a company will usually be something like a bespoke legal document, a computer program, a shipment of goods, and so on.

The *method used* refers, of course, to what you do to create that end product. This means the particular skills you have developed yourself: things such as templates, special short cuts or know-how. You might have built these things up over years, or learnt them on this particular project – and therein lies the problem. Where exactly did you gain these skills? How much was learnt on this particular job?

If you sell pure products it is easy. You own the IPR to both. If you have developed a one-off product or piece of work for a particular client it is a little different. In most cases, the fairest agreement for IPR will be that the client owns the IPR of the end product while your company retains the IPR of the methods used to produce that product. Here is an example of some legal wording that fits this scenario. It is taken from a contract to supply bespoke training courses but applies to most services:

The intellectual property rights in the course, and the copyright to it, shall vest in the client [i.e. the company that is buying the course.] All of the rights to the know-how, experience and skilled techniques in writing the course and providing the services shall vest in the supplier.

Sensible as this agreement may seem, you will probably be asked, from time to time, to make variations to it. There are two variations you will most commonly be asked to make.

➤ **Variation 1:** The prospect wants the IPR to the method used, as well as the end product. Prospects usually ask for this, not because they secretly covet your business, but because they do not understand the difference between 'methods used' and 'end product'. Therefore your first response should be to educate the prospect. Owning the IPR to methods used is a remarkably useless asset to your client. What use is the IPR of an obscure IT subsystem to high street retailer for example? Some customers insist on owning it, but if you give it away then you run the risk of being unable to consult in the future without paying royalties to your client.

➤ **Variation 2:** Your boss wants to keep the IPR of the end product for your company so that you can sell on the work later as your own product. If this situation applies to you the simplest thing is to change the wording in the contract you offer. Specifically you should change the word 'client' to 'supplier' in the clause described above. Alternatively you give the client free perpetual use of the product that is built, and any enhancements to it. This could well suit both parties, as the client is unlikely to have much interest in the intricacies of your profession.

E-mail

E-mail is a particularly beguiling form of communication. It is written in the manner of a casual conversation but has the permanence of a legal document.

When court cases loom, lawyers ask for the e-mail conversation 'threads' and find that, in most cases, the threads incriminate both parties. This happens because the issue being disputed usually 'emerged' during the e-mail conversation before both parties were on their guard to the legal implications of what they were writing.

What this all means is that if you have something to say that is of critical importance to the contract, you are better off saying it by letter, rather than by e-mail. The reasons are:

➤ Judges are from a generation that prefers letters to e-mail threads. Consequently they attach more weight to letters.

> A letter is separate from the e-mail threads, and so distances you from the incriminating things you may have typed there.

> A letter can wrong-foot the opposition because, remarkably, most modern companies are no longer set up to correspond by letter. Their replies will look sloppy if the matter goes to court.

If you do use e-mail to agree a contract, then you should formally and clearly confirm the agreement in a follow-up letter.

How can you avoid things going wrong when you are agreeing contracts?

Attending legal negotiations

If you are to attend a negotiation at which an opposing lawyer will be present you should meet with your lawyer beforehand. That will allow you to get advice from your lawyer and instruct them on your requirements so that each of you understands what issues are important and what can be traded. In-house lawyers should be the guard dogs of your firm and most will defend you stoutly. However, some of these legal guard dogs have temperaments that can turn on those they are meant to protect, so keep a special eye on your most junior staff. They will be the ones most at risk.

A pre-meeting also reduces two risks that otherwise exist in legal meetings:

> That your lawyer will dig their heels in on a point that is unimportant to you.

> That you will say something you shouldn't.

On a more positive note, a pre-meeting will help because there is a good chance the opposition will not have had one. Also, neither your lawyer nor the opposing lawyer is likely to have specialist knowledge of the subject being discussed – at least not to the level you have. If you use the pre-meeting to give your lawyer a thorough briefing you will be in a stronger position.

Whenever you go into a meeting like this you should have all the relevant paperwork to hand. This might sound obvious, but there are an amazing number of legal meetings, and court proceedings, in which this is a problem.

But what if the delivery starts before the contract is sorted?

Commercial pressures mean this happens a lot. And if trust between the two parties breaks down at this point the legal situation can be difficult. So what should you do if you find yourself in such a position? Well, your options are usually limited to the following:

> ➤ Make a commercial judgement as to how much delivery you can expose your company to without contract cover.

> ➤ Speed up the sorting of the legal side. When you are skating on thin ice, your safety lies in your speed.

> ➤ Agree a freeze on the delivery until contracts are signed.

There are no magic bullets here. You have to use your wits and your lightest feet.

So they have signed the contract!

The feeling you get having taken a sale from first contact through to close is wonderful. There are just a couple of things to remember at this point:

> ➤ Remember to thank your client for the work. (A remarkable number of salespeople do not.)

> ➤ Arrange to meet the customer at regular intervals in the future to ensure your company is still giving good service. Not only will this help ensure that good service is maintained, it will also give you visibility of new work that comes up (as it probably will).

And now there is just one more aspect of selling you need to know ...

Chapter **20**

So what makes the difference between average and top-flight sales performance?

- Motivation and goals
- The seven ways you can create luck

'Show me a man of average ability but extraordinary desire and I'll show you a winner every time.'

Andrew Carnegie (1835–1919), industrialist

You now know most of what can be known about the tips, tricks and techniques for selling. The next step is to apply this knowledge, day to day, until it becomes ingrained. Using this book as a reference will help greatly with that.

But comprehensive sales knowledge will only take you so far. What will take you the extra mile is motivation. In selling, motivation is to ability as three is to one.

So what creates motivation?

Many books portray motivation as a complex set of emotions but actually it only has two components: desire and hope. Nothing else. For a salesperson, hope means you need to believe you have a real chance of achieving your goals. As to desire, that has to come from within you. The most practical way to create and maintain your desire is to set some goals.

So what are your goals? When you get to the bottom of it, most people have the same three goals in their work. They are:

> a sense of well-being

> recognition

> money.

Most people put them in that order and find they need all three to really enjoy their work. The only real differences to the order occur in that a few people place more emphasis on the money, and a few extroverts place more emphasis on recognition.

That is what motivation is about. Desire and hope. Those drivers, plus the skills you have learnt from this book, will be enough to propel you to the very heights of sales. There is just one last thing you need ...

You need to create luck

To outsiders it seems that the best salespeople benefit from an abundant flow of good luck. It's true that some of them are naturally lucky people. The good news is that you can improve your selling luck a bit. As you might expect, there are seven ways in which you can do that. They are:

1 You will stumble into more opportunities if you are open, optimistic and ready to explore new experiences.

2　You should avoid spending time with the negative salespeople in your team. They will bring you down.

3　Remember that, in terms of morale, the best time to sell something is just after you have sold something. It's best to get straight on to the next customer.

4　You need to believe that everything, in the end, happens for the best.

5　You need to keep in tune with your intuition and your environment. That will help you pick up on opportunity.

6　You should expect to win, however much adversity you face.

7　You should persevere, however much adversity you face.

The salesperson has much the same role to a company as oil has to the workings of a machine. The oil is of no value in itself unless it is found on the contact surfaces of all parts. Then it brings great value.

You now know what the gold standard of selling is about. And that knowledge will stay with you for life. You will not need to make changes to that knowledge, because the rules of selling rarely change. And you now have the tips, tricks and techniques to win in any sales situation. What you need to do now is apply these rules and you will win. Some of your colleagues will wonder at the change.

Do you know of anyone who might also benefit from reading this book?

Would you like to know more?

Business books are a wonderful way to convey information and improve your results. Indeed, there are few better ways. But the information they contain will only benefit you if you retain the information and put the concepts into practice. Fortunately this book comes with features that help you do just that.

First, some parts of this book are available for free download from www.secrets-of-selling.com Some of these downloads are the things you tend to need at pressured times in the sales process, such as the proposal template. Others are things you cannot carry round in your head. For example, up-to-date lists of useful addresses for a wide range of sales and marketing activities.

Second, a course of the book has been developed by the author, working with one of the world's largest independent sales training companies. The course is specifically designed to maximise the knowledge that will be retained by your staff. It also allows your staff to work through examples and information from the book that specifically relate to their industry sector – something that will also benefit them greatly because it is so practical.

To find out more about this course please follow the link on the website or contact the training company direct at:

www.secrets-of-selling/training
Tel: ++44 (0)118 940 5123
Email: secretsofselling@pursuitnha.com
Courses are available in most countries and for almost all industry sectors.

Bibliography

Allen, D. (2004) *Ready for Anything* Piatkus

Argyle, M. (1990) *Bodily Communication* Routledge

Ashton, R. (2004) *How to Sell* Warner Business Books

Barry, A. (2002) *PR Power* Virgin Publishing

Bland, M., Theaker, A. and Wragg, D. (2000) *Effective Public Relations* Kogan Page

Braun, T. *The Philosophy of Branding* Kogan Page

Buchanan, D. and Huczynski, A. (1985) *Organizational Behaviour: An Introductory Text* Prentice Hall

Casse, P. (1995) *The One Hour Negotiator* Butterworth Heinemann

Chalker, S. and Weiner, E. (1994) *The Oxford Dictionary of English Grammar* Oxford University Press

Clutterbuck, D. and Kernaghan, S. (1991) *Making Customers Count* Mercury

Curzon, L. (2002) *Dictionary of Law* Pearson Longman

Delahunty, A. and Weiner, J. (1994) *The Oxford Guide to English Usage* Oxford University Press

Dembitz, A. and Essinger, J. (2000) *Breakthrough Consulting* FT Prentice Hall

Denny, R. (2001) *Selling to Win* Kogan Page

Drucker, P. (2002) *Managing in the New Society* Butterworth Heinemann

Fisher, R. and Ury, W. (1991) *Getting to Yes* Business Books

Forsyth, P. (2002) *Successful Negotiation* How To Books

Gates, B. (2000) *Business at the Speed of Thought* Penguin

Guirdham, M. (1990) *Interpersonal Skills at Work* Prentice Hall

Haig, M. (2003) *Brand Failures* Kogan Page

Harris, S. (1990) *Human Communications* Blackwell Publishing

Hart, N. (1993) *The Practice of Advertising* Butterworth Heinemann

Hart, N. (1995) *The Practice of Selling* Butterworth Heinemann

Henley, N. (1977) *Body Politics: Power, Sex and Nonverbal Communication* Prentice Hall

Hess, E. (1965) 'Attitudes and pupil size' *Scientific American*

Kapferer, J. (2001) *Reinventing the Brand* Kogan Page

Keenan, D. and Riches, S. (2005) *Business Law* Pearson Longman

Kent, R. (1993) *Market Research in Action* Routledge

Lancaster, G. and Jobber, D. (2003) *Selling and Sales Management* FT Prentice Hall

Lewis, H. (2004) *Consultants and Advisers* Kogan Page

MaCrae, C. (1991) *World Class Brands* Addison Wesley

Martin, J. (2005) *The English Legal System* Hodder Arnold

McDonald, M. (1997) *Marketing Plans* Butterworth Heinemann

McKenna, E. (1987) *Psychology in Business: Theory and Applications* Erlbaum Associates

Nash, S. (2005) *The Successful Consultant* How To Books

Newent, T. (1992) *Advertising in Britain* Heinemann

Peatie, K. (1992) *Green Marketing* Pitman

Plait, R. (1999) *ecommerce* FT Prentice Hall

Senge, P. (2003) *The Fifth Discipline* Nicholas Brealey Publishing

Shaw, R. (1993) *Computer Aided Marketing and Selling* Butterworth Heinemann

Shea, M. (1988) *The Primary Effect* Orion Business Books

Sheldon Green, P. (1995) *Winning PR Tactics* Pitman Publishing

Singer, B. (2001) *Sales Dogs* Warner Business Books

Smith, J. (2000) *30 Minutes to Make the Right Decision* Kogan Page

Sutherland, K. (1991) *Researching Business Markets* Kogan Page

Rackham, N. (1989) *Major Account Sales Strategy* McGraw Hill

Randall, G. (1997) *Branding* Kogan Page

Robbins, S. (2003) *The Truth About Managing People* FT Prentice Hall

Robinson, C. (1995) *Effective Negotiation* Kogan Page

Timperley, J. (2004) *Network Your Way to Success* Piatkus

Tzu, S. (1971) *The Art of War,* Oxford University Press

Weitz, B. and Wensley, R. (2002) *Handbook of Marketing* Sage

West, M. (2004) *Effective Teamwork* BPS Blackwell

Index